SMALL UNIT ACTION IN VIETNAM SUMMER 1966

By

Captain Francis J. West, Jr., USMCR

HISTORY AND MUSEUMS DIVISION
HEADQUARTERS, U. S. MARINE CORPS
WASHINGTON, D. C.
Printed 1967
Reprinted 1977

TABLE OF CONTENTS

	Page
Foreword.	1
Mines and Men.	3
Units involved: 9th Marines; 3d Amphibian Tractor Battalion; MAG-36.	
Howard's Hill.	15
Units involved: 1st Reconnaissance Battalion; 5th Marines; MAG-11; MAG-12; MAG-36	
No Cigar.	31
Units involved: 5th Marines.	
Night Action.	46
Units involved: 7th Marines.	
The Indians.	59
Units involved: 1st Force Reconnaissance Company; 12th Marines; MAG-11.	
Talking Fish.	68
Units involved: 12th Marines.	
An Honest Effort.	77
Units involved: 5th Marines.	
A Hot Walk in the Sun.	82
Units involved: 5th Marines; 1st Engineer Battalion; Provisional Scout Dog Platoon; MAG-36.	
"General, We Killed Them".	90
Units involved: 5th Marines; 9th Engineer Battalion; Provisional Scout Dog Platoon; MAG-12; MAG-36.	
Glossary of Marine Small Arms.	122

FOREWORD

The origin of this pamphlet lies in the continuing program at all levels of command to keep Marines informed of the ways of combat and civic action in Vietnam. Not limited in any way to set methods and means, this informational effort spreads across a wide variety of projects, all aimed at making the lessons learned in Vietnam available to the Marine who is fighting there and the Marine who is soon due to take his turn in combat.

Recognizing a need to inform the men who are the key to the success of Marine Corps operations--the enlisted Marines and junior officers of combat and combat support units--the former Assistant Chief of Staff, G-3, Major General William R. Collins, originated a project to provide a timely series of short, factual narratives of small unit action, stories which would have lessons learned as an integral part. Essential to General Collins' concept was the fact that the stories would have to be both highly readable and historically accurate. The basic requirement called for an author trained in the methodology of research, with recent active duty experience at the small unit level in the FMF, and a proven ability to write in a style that would ensure wide readership.

On the recommendation of retired Brigadier General Frederick P. Henderson, Captain Francis J. West, Jr., a Marine reserve officer, was invited to apply for assignment to active duty during the summer of 1966 to research and write the small unit action stories. Captain West was well qualified to undertake the project: he had recently been on active duty as a platoon leader in the Special Landing Force in the Western Pacific; he had majored in history as an undergraduate at Georgetown University and was a graduate student at the Woodrow Wilson School of Public and International Affairs at Princeton University; and he had written a number of articles, papers, and a book which indicated that he had the capability of communicating with a wide and varied audience.

Recalled to active duty at his own request late in May 1966, Captain West was given a series of informal briefings at Headquarters Marine Corps on the current situation in Vietnam and was soon on his way to that country. He arrived at Da Nang on 5 June and went into the field immediately as an observer/member of a wide variety of Marine small units and saw action in all parts of the III Marine Amphibious Force area of responsibility. Developing his own methods of operation, and carrying in addition to normal weapons and equipment, a tape recorder, a camera, and a note pad, the captain took part in most of the actions he describes and interviewed participants in the others immediately after the events portrayed. During his stay in Vietnam, Captain West was actively supported in his work by the Marines with whom he served, and by none more helpfully than the III MAF commander, Lieutenant General Lewis W. Walt, and his G-3, Colonel John R. Chaisson, who read and approved each of the rough draft narratives that Captain West completed in Vietnam. Colonel Thomas M. Fields, of the Combat Information Bureau at Da Nang, also provided much assistance and support.

This pamphlet, then, is based upon first-hand, eye-witness accounting of the events described. It is documented by notes and taped interviews taken in the field and includes lessons learned from the mouths of the Marines who are currently fighting in Vietnam. It is published for the information of those men who are serving and who will serve in Vietnam, as well as for the use of other interested Americans, so that they may better understand the demands of the Vietnam conflict on the individual Marine.

R. L. MURRAY
Major General, U. S. Marine Corps
Assistant Chief of Staff, G-3

REVIEWED AND APPROVED: 5 January 1967

MINES AND MEN

<u>Preface</u>: The author spent two weeks with the 9th Marines, most of the time with Delta Company. He participated in the patrol described as an extra infantryman, swapping his tape recorder for an automatic rifle when the platoon was hit. Throughout most of the fight, he did not see the patrol leader, but later was able to piece together the entire action by interviews and by listening to his recorder, which was running throughout the engagement.

In late spring and early summer of 1966, the most notorious area in I Corps was the flat rice paddy-and-hedgerow complex around Hill 55, seven miles southwest of Da Nang. In the Indochina War, two battalions of the French forces were wiped out on Hill 55; in the Vietnam War, a Marine lieutenant colonel was killed on the same hill. The 9th Marines had the responsibility for clearing the area and no one envied the regimental commander, Colonel Edwin Simmons, and his men their job. The enemy they hated, the enemy they feared the most, the enemy they found hardest to combat, was not the VC; it was mines.

One company of the regiment--Delta--lost 10 KIA and 58 WIA in five weeks. Two men were hit by small arms fire, one by a grenade. Mines inflicted all the other casualties. Only four of the wounded returned to duty. From a peak strength of 175, Delta Company dropped to 120 effectives. Among those evacuated or killed were a high percentage of the company's leaders: five platoon commanders; three platoon sergeants; nine squad leaders; and six fire team leaders.

On 8 May, the 1st Platoon of Delta Company was 52 men strong, commanded by a first lieutenant and honchoed* by a staff sergeant. For a month they patrolled. At division level, the operations section could see a pattern which indicated the patrols were slowly and surely rooting the VC infrastructure out of the area. But for the individual rifleman, it was ugly, unrewarding work. The VC in previous encounters had learned the futility of determined engagements against the Marines. So they sniped and ran and left behind the mines.

---

*honcho - Marine slang, derived from Japanese, for a boss.

On 8 June, the 1st Platoon prepared to go out on another patrol. By then, they numbered 32 men and were commanded by a sergeant.

During patrols on the previous day there had been no casualties. Far from feeling encouraged, the troops were pessimistic, believing it inevitable that today another of their group would step on a mine.

Captain John Hart had commanded Delta Company for nine months, and another company in Vietnam before that. A shrewd tactician with a natural ease and understanding of his men, the red-headed company commander had decided to send two amtracs* with the platoon to set off the mines before the troops reached them.

Sergeant William Cunningham believed the amtracs would solve his problem. They would cruise through the flat lowlands, smashing mined fences and tearing up known minefields. The platoon would walk in the tracks of the 35-ton amtracs, unless forced by fire to disperse or ordered to do otherwise. A 60mm mortar would deal with the snipers, who were more bothersome than dangerous. The plan seemed sound.

The patrol moved out in two columns in the wake of an amtrac. The platoon members knew the area well. They hated it. The paddies and fields stretched for miles in checkerboard fashion, separated by thick tree lines and numerous hamlets. The mud of the rice paddies clung like glue to boots. The numerous tree lines could be penetrated only by using machetes and axes. The scattered hamlets contained from 1 to 10 houses and each house was surrounded by thorn fences harder to break than barbed wire. The level ground prevented a man from seeing beyond the next hedgerow.

And everywhere the mines. There seemed to be no pattern to their emplacement. They had been scattered at trail junctions, at the intersection of rice dikes, along fences, under gates. Having watched the movements of Marine patrols in this area, the enemy buried their mines where they anticipated the Marines would walk. Often they scouted the direction and path a patrol was taking and planted the mines ahead. If the patrol passed that point safely, the VC would scurry out of his hiding place, dig up his mine, and keep it for another day.

Sergeant Cunningham was aware of this fact. By the same route he had used the day before, he was returning to the same hamlet complex so that the amtracs could set off the mines. The enemy's supply of mines was not inexhaustible,

---

* Amtrac - Marine slang for Amphibious Landing Vehicle, Tracked (LVT).

An LVT of the 3d Amphibian Tractor Battalion, similar to those that supported Sergeant Cunningham's platoon, moves out through a column of infantrymen (USMC A184999)

especially since most were M16 "Bouncing Betties"*, captured from the ARVNs**. This was one way of destroying them. Before the platoon left the patrol base, the sergeant repeatedly warned his men to stay in the tracks of the LVTs.

The Marines wore helmets and flak jackets***. Each rifleman carried 150 rounds of ammunition and 2 or more hand grenades. The men of the two machine gun crews were draped with belts of linked cartridges totalling 1,200 rounds. The two 3.5-inch rocket launcher teams carried five high explosive (HE) and five white phosphorus (WP) rockets. Four grenadiers carried 28 40mm shells apiece for their stubby M79s. Sergeant Cunningham had given six LAAWs**** to some riflemen to provide additional area target capability. Artillery and mortars were on call. The 2d Platoon would range within 1,000 yards of Sergeant Cunningham's men at all times. Although Cunningham believed the platoon would draw only harassing fire, Captain Hart never allowed his men to patrol without ensuring heavy firepower. Similarly, the battalion commander, Lieutenant Colonel Richard E. Jones, liked his company commanders to arrange for their patrols to have on-call artillery concentrations whenever possible.

The platoon moved out at 1100. There was no breeze and no shade. The temperature was 102 degrees. Within five minutes, every Marine was soaked in sweat. The column plodded south, strung out over a quarter of a mile. There was no flank section, such was the fear of mines and the confidence in quick support, if needed. One amtrac was in the lead; the second stayed back 200 yards in the middle of the column.

After marching for half of an hour, Sergeant Cunningham halted the column. Directly in front of the lead amtrac a thorn and bamboo fence ran at right angles to the line of march. Two hundred meters to the right front lay a thick tree line in which the thatch rooftops of four houses could be seen. To the left a dirt field stretched for 400 meters, stopping at another tree line. Other tree lines lay at farther distances to the front and rear.

Sergeant Cunningham had seen his radioman and one of his squad leaders trip a mine attached to that fence and die. Yesterday he had cautiously led his platoon across the fence and had been fired at. Today, with obvious satisfaction and

---

*Bouncing Betty - Marine slang for antipersonnel mine which explodes in midair.
**ARVNs - Marine slang for soldiers of the Army of the Republic of Vietnam
***flak jacket - Marine slang for individual body armor.
****LAAW - Marine slang for portable antitank weapon; see Glossary of Weapons.

relief, he yelled to the lead tractor: "Rip that thing apart. Really tear it up."

The driver turned left so that the amtrac could hit the fence head-on. It lumbered forward, crushing 30 feet of fence before its left track slipped into a drainage ditch. The LVT churned to a halt. The second amtrac eased forward, attached a tow rope to the front of the stranded vehicle, and pulled it out.

Sergeant Cunningham decided to continue south to the minefields and tear other holes in the fence on the return trip that afternoon. "Move out," he shouted, "We'll come back to that bear later on. It'll still be here." One amtrac roared ahead while the second idled by the fence, waiting to turn into position near the center of the column.

The hard dirt around the fence had been churned into jagged clods by the treads of the two amtracs. The point Marines, including Sergeant Cunningham, carefully picked their way across the fence, stepping only in the tracks, and fell in trace again behind the lead LVT. The rest of the column followed.

Cunningham had walked fifty meters away from the fence when he heard the explosion. Even before he turned his head he knew what he would see. A thick black cloud hung in the air beside the fence line. Three Marines were sprawled on the ground. Before the shower of loose dirt and shrapnel had stopped falling, the platoon's senior corpsman, Hospitalman 3d Class Robert E. Perkins, had reached the side of the most seriously wounded Marine.

Corporal Raymond Lewis, leading the point squad, burst out: "Hey, why the hell don't they follow the goddamn tracks?" Sergeant Cunningham raced back, yelling in anger and frustration and hurt, "I told you to follow me through here, here--we came through here." A pause, then, in a resigned voice: "O.K. Who got it?"

Tired, feeling secure because there were many tracks near the fence and nine Marines had walked safely past, the tenth Marine had wandered off the path of the treads. For 20 feet he had been following the dry trail of old tank treads. The VC had placed a mine on the old trail resting against the torn fence. The Marine had tripped a Bouncing Betty mine, which flew knee-high before it exploded, felling him and two Marines behind him.

The column had halted, well spread out but near no cover or concealment. The platoon's leaders were clustered at the fence checking the wounded.

Then the sniping started. The first four to eight rounds were ignored by the entire column. The Marines received fire every day. When asked one hour earlier if he expected fire on the patrol, Sergeant Cunningham had flatly stated that he did. The Marines were not going to divert attention from their wounded because they received some random incoming rounds.

Ten seconds later, the situation changed abruptly. The sniping became steady fire and the targets were the wounded, the platoon leaders, and the platoon radioman. The enemy had found the range and the wounded could hear the whine and snap of close misses.

Disregarding the firing, Sergeant Cunningham and the platoon guide, Sergeant Peter Hastings, continued to discuss the technical details necessary as they called for an immediate helicopter evacuation of the wounded. The platoon radioman, Private First Class Blas Falcon, stood with them taking notes. Perkins worked swiftly to prevent the most seriously wounded Marine from bleeding to death. He did not even look up from his probing of the man's legs when the bullets started passing close by. He had been with the company for nine days and had tended exactly nine Marines wounded by mines.

Most of the fire was coming from a hamlet on the west flank of the platoon, not more than 200 meters to the right of the point squad. Some was coming from the distant tree line to the left. Among the enemy weapons, the Marines could distinguish the flat, low reports of several carbines from the sharp sound of an M1. A light machine gun began shooting short bursts. Harassment had become engagement.

The VC had carefully planned the trap. The mine had stopped the column in the open less than 200 meters from their firing position. To confuse and spread the Marines, they had posted snipers on the other flank. They knew the leaders would cluster around the wounded. They had their weapons sighted in on the fence line. No more than 20 seconds had passed since the VC had opened fire. They had much better positions and had gained fire superiority from the start.

The volume of enemy fire increased so rapidly Cunningham never had a chance to contact his three squad leaders and issue any comprehensive order. The initial response was a matter of individual initiative, as Marines flopped down and began returning fire without waiting for orders. But their fire was ragged and scattered, lacking direction and purpose.

Corporal Lewis directed the first determined, collective effort to destroy the enemy. Having moved out in front of the column, the 1st Squad was 100 meters ahead of the main body.

Lewis' five men were heavily armed and he used all the weapons he had at his command. Over the din of the increasing volume of incoming fire, he could not hear Sergeant Cunningham. But he did not need to be told what to do. Lewis had been fighting in Vietnam for eight months and had participated in dozens of fire fights. Flattened out along the side of the trail, his squad was not under fire but was nearest to the hamlet. To his left front he could hear the crack of sniper rifles coming from a tree line. Quickly, he directed his machine gunner to set up and rake the far tree line, keeping his fire low and continuous. The squad grenadier, Private First Class Michael Stay, was pumping 40mm shells into the hamlet as fast as he could fire and reload. Lewis decided to add more punch.

He turned his bazooka team toward the hamlet. The team leader, Corporal John Martin, had anticipated his squad leader. His rocket launcher was set and ready to fire. The men agreed on the targets: the houses. Both had seen men firing from raised flaps on the roofs. Martin placed the long tube on his shoulder, sighted swiftly, and fired from a kneeling position. A house shuddered and pitched at an angle. He placed another white phosporous rocket in the launcher and fired. A second house burst into flames. He reloaded and fired again. The third house exploded. The enemy machine gun stopped. Another rocket and a LAAW were fired into the tree line. Lewis, Martin, and Lance Corporal Dennis Sullivan lay prone and began firing their M14 rifles at the hedgerows bordering the huts. The fire fight was less than 2 minutes old.

The 60mm mortar crew took up where Martin left off. Sergeant James Gibbs and his two crew members had been riding on the second LVT. When the enemy machine gun fired, they jumped off the tractor and yelled to Cunningham, "Should we try for the gun?"

"Go ahead," Cunningham yelled back, "but watch it when the choppers get here."

Less than 300 meters from the hamlet, the crew set up their small tube. Gibbs aimed in by line of sight while Lance Corporal Joe Dykes estimated the range and Private First Class Peter Vidaurie hauled ammunition from the amtrac. "Can we fire now?" yelled Gibbs.

"Sure, any time you want," replied Cunningham.

For the next two minutes, the 60mm crew walked rounds back and forth along the 200-meter length of the tree line. Under cover of this shooting, Sergeant Cunningham directed his 2d Squad into position to secure a landing zone for the helicopters. He wanted to get his wounded out before the enemy machine gun resumed firing.

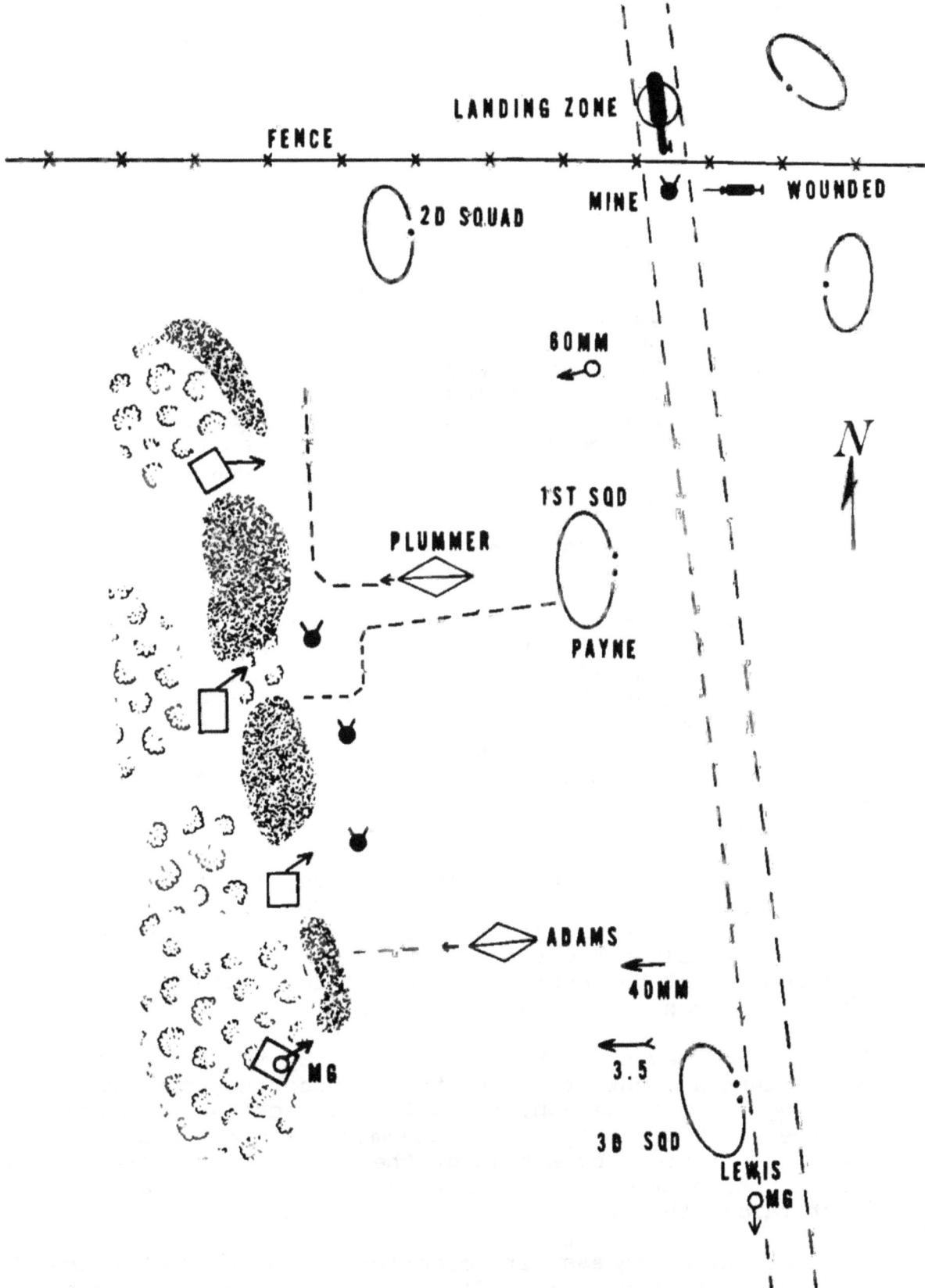

SCHEMATIC SKETCH TO ACCOMPANY "MINES AND MEN"

"Come on, the hell with waiting for this thing," an angry Marine yelled, gesturing at the amtrac, "let's go get them!" Payne grabbed him by the shoulder as he started around the tractor's side. "No, you don't. That whole field is mined. They're just trying to sucker you in. Stay behind the trac!"

One hundred meters to the left, Adams' amtrac had already reached the hedgerow and was smashing its way into the hamlet. That decided Plummer. His tractor crawled up the embankment and pitched down into the level field and rumbled toward the village. A Marine followed right behind. Payne yelled, "We're going in." The five Marines clustered around him nodded nervously and said nothing. They were more than a little apprehensive. They would follow but they wanted somebody to lead. Payne scrambled up the embankment into a burst of machine gun fire. His helmet spun off and he pitched forward head first. The squad froze. Payne was their leader, the most experienced man, the one who knew what to do. They thought he was dead.

Payne got up, unhurt but shaken. "Come on," he muttered. They dogtrotted across the field after the amtrac.

By that time Adams' amtrac had entered the tree line. Lewis ordered his squad to cease fire. The amtrac passed the house where Adams had fired at the sniper hiding in the roof. Private First Class Larry Blume, a demolition engineer riding in the LVT, saw two men run from the house to the left. But he couldn't get a shot at them. Adams was watching out the observer's window, placed to the right of the driver's seat. He saw a VC, trying to dodge across the path of the tractor, stumble and fall. The amtrac crushed him.

Plummer's LVT had reached the tree line and the thorn fence surrounding the village. The sergeant turned his vehicle right to avoid the flames. The Marines peeled off left and ran along the fence line looking for an opening. They went in at the center of the village. The point Marine hesitated, then turned to the right.

Payne knew that the machine gun lay to their left but he too turned right, thinking that, since the point man was ignoring the machine gun, he must be attacking another target. But the point did not know of the machine gun. His sudden appearance behind the amtrac at the start of the assault had caught the enemy machine gunner by surprise. Payne was the first target the machine gunner had fired at.

So while the assault force rushed to the right, the VC slipped out to the left. Adams saw six of them moving toward his amtrac, four dragging two bodies. He couldn't fire the .30 caliber machine gun for fear of hitting the Marine squad sweeping in the other direction. Nor could he pursue them through the burning village. The tractor broke out of the tree line on the far side of the hamlet, pivoted right, and raced along a cane field to turn the assault troops. The VC slipped away toward the left flank.

While the assault was going in, the wounded Marines were lying where they had fallen, joking with Hastings and Falcon. Helicopters had been called and they knew they would soon be under expert care. At all times helicopters sat on the Da Nang airstrip, 16 miles to the rear, ready to evacuate the wounded, like ambulances at city hospitals--only faster.

Eight minutes had elapsed since the wounded had fallen, and circling overhead, looking for the green smoke grenade which signalled a secure landing zone, were two Hueys*. Hastings threw the grenade and down clattered one chopper. The other circled aloft, ready to pounce on any enemy firing position. That capability was not needed. The landing zone was very secure. The 3d Squad was pushing the enemy out of the hamlet. Cunningham had settled the fire teams of the 2d Squad in the outskirts of the surrounding tree lines, ready to stifle by fire any enemy who tried to down the Huey. Still, a fight was raging and one of the wounded became concerned that the helicopter might choose not to land. "Give me a rifle," he said, "I'll secure this damn landing zone myself, if it means I get out of here afterwards."

The helicopter settled in. Hastings was extremely careful to bring the Huey down right on the tracks of the amtracs so it would not detonate another mine. The wounded were placed on board, and the helicopter took off, headed for "Charlie Med"** receiving hospital. Thirteen minutes after the mine had exploded, the wounded were being tended by doctors and receiving transfusions. All would live.

The assault force was running again. Adams had told them they were going the wrong way. They had stopped, gasped for breath, and stumbled out the back of the village in trace of the amtrac. A trench line ran from the village to another tree line and hamlet 400 meters in the rear of the burned village. Beside this trench the eight Marines trotted. They had no more sweat to drop. Most had burns where their hands or arms had accidently brushed the heated rifle barrels. Their flak jackets and helmets weighted them down. They didn't ease up.

---

*Huey - Marine slang for UH1E helicopter.
**Charlie Med - Marine slang for Company C of a medical battalion.

Two hundred meters from the tree line, Payne croaked to his machine gun team to drop off and cover their advance. The LVT stopped at the tree line and readied its machine gun. The Marines swept into the village by pairs, covering the advance of each other. The village was empty. The trench line was empty. The numerous fighting holes were empty. Punji traps and bamboo stakes were everywhere. It was a typical VC village.

The Marines turned back, withdrawing cautiously, thoroughly exhausted. Cunningham joined them near the machine gun emplacement, bringing the two squads and the other tractor with him. Adams and Blume told the sergeant where they had seen the VC and the bodies. Cunningham was puzzled. He said he had passed that area five minutes after the amtracs and had seen only women, children, and old men fleeing to the left flank. He had seen no VC and no bodies. In that short time lapse either the VCs, or the villagers (probably relatives)-- or both--had policed the battlefield.

Cunningham consolidated his position and sent engineers into the village to blow the bunkers and trench lines. The entire action lasted less than 40 minutes. Within six minutes the assault had been launched. Not one Marine was wounded in the attack. It was sudden and fierce and took the VC by surprise. The Marines were surprised themselves. In seven months in Vietnam, Payne had never before charged the enemy. Nor had his men.

The action was sharp, brief, and inconclusive. The assault force, assuming the VC would pull directly back, had been badly fooled by the enemy's flank escape, probably by use of tunnels or trenches. Carelessness and inattention caused the mine casualties, as they had caused many before and would continue to do so. The middle men of a patrol on the march under a hot sun had tended to relax and shuffle along.

On the other hand, the platoon responded to fire like veterans (which they were, most having over four months of combat patrolling). In some cases (Corporal Lewis and Private First Class Adams stand out) initial initiative was impressive. The number of Marines returning fire was almost total. Thirty-nine men were engaged in the action; 33 fired their weapons, either individual or team. Those not firing were the platoon commander, the platoon corpsman, the platoon radio man, and the three wounded. The area fire weapons--the 3.5s, the LAAWs, and the M79s--were particularly effective in reducing the volume of enemy fire.

The platoon commander and the squad leaders moved swiftly but not rashly. They covered their flanks and did not commit the entire platoon at one time in one bunched movement, thus minimizing the chance of a successful ambush. Lewis covered the amtracs and then Payne's squad when they rushed the village. Cunningham had one more squad backing Lewis. Payne covered his pursuit objective with his machine gun team and the amtrac. Cunningham had on call at all times 81mm mortars and artillery; Gibbs' 60mm mortar was well supplied with ammunition.

The physical conditioning of the entire platoon was superior. They ran, fought, and thought in intense heat, no mean accomplishment.

The Marines had cleared the field by firepower and aggressive maneuver. They had hurt the VC but did not know how badly. The mine had severely wounded one Marine and put two more out of action. During the remainder of the day no sniper fired at the platoon. That was unusual. The next day, the company suffered no casualties and received very light incoming fire--that too was unusual. The following day, a Marine from the 3d Platoon in the middle of a column tripped a mine and five Marines were evacuated. The harassing fire that day was moderately heavy, inaccurate, and delivered at long range. That was usual.

HOWARD'S HILL

Preface: The author was on another patrol the night of the Howard fight. He met with the men of Charlie Company, who relieved Howard's platoon, immediately upon their return and taped their comments and reactions. Then he went to the hospital at Chulai and interviewed Howard and his men, talking later with the pilots, the Special Forces officers, and Howard's company and battalion commanders. The pictures--the only ones taken on the hill during the fight--were provided by First Lieutenant Philip Freed, who was the Forward Air Controller with Charlie Company.

The Marine Corps has a tested tradition: it will never leave alone on the field of combat one of its fighting men. It will go to fantastic lengths and commit to battle scores of men to aid and protect a few. This is the story of a few such Marines, of the battle they fought, and the help they received from all the services, not just the Marine Corps.

Some 20 miles inland to the west of the Marine base at Chulai runs a range of steep mountains and twisting valleys. In that bandits' lair, the Viet Cong and North Vietnamese could train and plan for attacks against the heavily populated seacoast hamlets, massing only when it was time to attack. In early June of 1966, the intelligence reports reaching III MAF headquarters indicated that a mixed force of Viet Cong and North Vietnamese was gathering by the thousands in those mountains. But the enemy leaders were not packing their troops into a few large, vulnerable assembly points; they kept their units widely dispersed, moving mainly in squads and platoons.

To frustrate that scheme and keep the enemy off balance, the Marines launched Operation KANSAS, an imaginative concept in strategy. Rather than send full infantry battalions to beat the bushes in search of small enemy bands, Lieutenant General Lewis W. Walt detailed the reconnaissance battalion of the 1st Marine Division to scout the mountains. The reconnaissance Marines would move in small teams of 8 to 20 men. If they located a large enemy concentration, Marine infantry would be flown in. If, as was expected, they saw only numerous small groups of Viet Cong and North Vietnamese, they were to smash them by calling in air and artillery strikes.

Lieutenant Colonel Arthur J. Sullivan had set high training standards for his battalion. Every man had received individual schooling in forward observer techniques and reconnaissance patrol procedures. He was confident his men could perform the mission successfully, despite the obvious hazards. "The Vietnam war," he said, "has given the small-unit leader--the corporal, the sergeant, the lieutenant--a chance to be independent. The senior officers just can't be out there looking over their shoulders. You have to have confidence in your junior officers and NCOs."

One such NCO was Staff Sergeant Jimmie Earl Howard, acting commander of the 1st Platoon, Charlie Company, 1st Reconnaissance Battalion. A tall, well-built man in his mid-thirties, Howard had been a star football player and later a coach at the San Diego Recruit Depot. Leadership came naturally to him. "Howard was a very personable fellow," his company commander, Captain Tim Geraghty said. "The men liked him. They liked to work for him." In Korea he had been wounded three times and awarded the Silver Star for bravery. In Vietnam he would receive a fourth Purple Heart and be recommended for the Medal of Honor.

As dusk fell on the evening of 13 June 1966, a flight of helicopters settled on the slope of Hill 488, 25 miles west of Chulai. Howard and his 17 men jumped out and climbed the steep incline to the top. The hill, called Nui Vu, rose to a peak of nearly 1,500 feet and dominated the terrain for miles. Three narrow strips of level ground ran along the top for several hundred yards before falling abruptly away. Seen from the air, they roughly resembled the three blades on an airplane propeller. Howard chose the blade which pointed north for his command post and placed observation teams on the other two blades. It was an ideal vantage point.

The enemy knew it also. Their foxholes dotted the ground, each with a small shelter scooped out two feet under the surface. Howard permitted his men use of these one-man caves during the day to avoid the hot sun and enemy detection. There was no other cover or concealment to be found. There were no trees, only knee-high grass and small scrub growth.

In the surrounding valleys and villages, there were many enemy. For the next two days, Howard was constantly calling for fire missions, as members of the platoon saw small enemy groups almost every hour. Not all the requests for air and artillery strikes were honored. Sullivan was concerned lest the platoon's position, so salient and bare, be spotted by a suspicious enemy. Most of the firing at targets located by the platoon was done only when there was an observation plane circling in the vicinity to decoy the enemy. After two days Sullivan and his executive officer, Major Allan Harris, became alarmed at the risk involved in leaving the platoon stationary any longer. But the observation post was ideal; Howard had encountered no difficulty, and, in any case, thought he had a secure escape route along a ridge to the east. So it was decided to leave the platoon on Nui Vu for one more day.

However, the enemy were well aware of the platoon's presence. (Sullivan has a theory that the Viet Cong and North Vietnamese, long harassed, disrupted, and punished by reconnaissance units in territory they claimed to control absolutely, had determined to eliminate one such unit, hoping thereby to demoralize the others. Looked at in hindsight, the ferocity and tenacity of the attack upon Nui Vu gives credence to the colonel's theory.) In any case, the North Vietnamese made their preparations well and did not tip their hand. On 15 June, they moved a fresh, well-equipped, highly trained battalion to the base of Nui Vu. In late afternoon hundreds of the enemy started to climb up the three blades, hoping to annihilate the dozen and a half Marines in one surprise attack.

The Army Special Forces frustrated that plan. Sergeant 1st Class Donald Reed and Specialist 5th Class Hardey Drande were leading a platoon of CIDG (Civilian Irregular Defense Group) forces on patrol near Nui Vu that same afternoon. They saw elements of the North Vietnamese battalion moving towards the hill and radioed the news back to their base camp at Hoi An, several miles to the south. Howard's radio was purposely set on the same frequency and so he was alerted at the same time. Reed and Drande wanted to hit the enemy from the rear and disrupt them, but had to abandon the idea when they suddenly found themselves a very unpopular minority of two on the subject. Describing the reactions of the Special Forces NCOs later, Howard could not resist chuckling. "The language those sergeants used over the radio," he said, "when they realized they couldn't attack the PAVNs*, well, they sure didn't learn it at communications school." Even though the Special Forces were not able to provide the ground support they wished to, their warning alerted Howard and enabled him to develop a precise defensive plan before the attack was launched.

Acting on the report, Howard gathered his team leaders, briefed them on the situation, selected an assembly point, instructed them to stay on full alert and to withdraw to the main position at the first sign of an approaching enemy. The corporals and lance corporals crept back to their teams and briefed them in the growing dusk. The Marines then settled down to watch and wait.

Lance Corporal Ricardo Binns had placed his observation team on the slope 40 meters forward of Howard's position. At

---

*PAVNs - Marine slang for soldiers of the Peoples' Army of (North) Vietnam.

approximately 2200, while the four Marines were lying in a shallow depression discussing in whispers their sergeant's solemn warnings, Binns quite casually propped himself up on his elbows and placed his rifle butt in his shoulder. Without saying a word, he pointed the barrel at a bush and fired. The bush pitched backward and fell thrashing 12 feet away.

The other Marines jumped up. Each threw a grenade, before grabbing his rifle and scrambling up the hill. Behind them grenades burst and automatic weapons pounded away. The battle of Nui Vu was on.

The other outposts withdrew to the main position. The Marines commanded a tiny rock-strewn knoll. The rocks would provide some protection for the defenders. Placing his two radios behind a large boulder, Howard set up a tight circular perimeter, not over 20 meters in diameter, and selected a firing position for each Marine.

The North Vietnamese too were setting up. They had made no audible noises while climbing. There was no talking, no clumsy movements. When Binns killed one of their scouts, they were less than 50 meters from the top.

The Marines were surrounded. From all sides the enemy threw grenades. Some bounced off the rocks; some rolled back down the slopes; some did not explode, but some landed right on Marines and did explode. The next day the platoon corpsman, Billie Don Holmes, recalled: "They were within twenty feet of us. Suddenly there were grenades all over. Then people started hollering. It seemed everyone got hit at the same time.

Holmes crawled forward to help. A grenade exploded between him and a wounded man. Holmes lost consciousness.

The battle was going well for the North Vietnamese. Four .50 caliber machine guns were firing in support of the assault units, their heavy explosive projectiles arcing in from the four points of the compass. Red tracer rounds from light machine guns streaked toward the Marine position, pointing the direction for reinforcements gathering in the valley. 60mm mortar shells smashed down and added rock splinters to the metal shrapnel whining through the air.

The North Vietnamese followed up the grenade shower with a full, well-coordinated assault, directed and controlled by shrill whistles and the clacking of bamboo sticks. From different directions, they rushed the position at the same time, firing automatic weapons, throwing grenades, and screaming. Howard later said he hadn't been sure how his troops would react. They were young and the situation looked hopeless.

They had been shocked and confused by the ferocity of the attack and the screams of their own wounded.

But they reacted savagely. The first lines of enemy skirmishers were cut down seconds after they stood up and exposed themselves. The assault failed to gain momentum any place and the North Vietnamese in the rearward ranks had more sense than to copy the mistakes of the dead. Having failed in their swift charge, they went to earth and probed the perimeter, seeking a weak spot through which they could drive. To do this, small bands of the enemy tried to crawl quite close to a Marine, then overwhelm him with a burst of fire and several grenades.

But the Marines too used grenades and the American hand grenade contains twice the blast and shrapnel effect of the Chinese Communist stick grenade. The Marines could throw farther and more accurately than the enemy. A Marine would listen for a movement, gauge the direction and distance, pull the pin, and throw. High pitched howls and excited jabberings mingled with the blasts. The North Vietnamese pulled back to regroup.

Howard had taken the PRC-25 radio from one of his communicators, Corporal Robert Lewis Martinez, and during the lull contacted Captain Geraghty and Lieutenant Colonel Sullivan. With his escape route cut off and his force facing overwhelming odds, Howard kept his message simple. "You've gotta get us out of here," he said. "There are too many of them for my people."

Sullivan tried. Because of his insistence upon detailed preplanning of extraction and fire support contingencies, he was a well-known figure at the Direct Air Support Center of the 1st Marine Division and when he called near midnight, he did not bandy words. He wanted flare ships, helicopters, and fixed wing aircraft dispatched immediately to Nui Vu.

Somehow, the response was delayed. And shortly after midnight, the enemy forces gathered and rushed forward in strength a second time. The Marines threw the last of their grenades and fired their rifles semiautomatically, relying on accuracy to suppress volume. It did and the enemy fell back, but by that time every Marine had been wounded.

The living took the ammunition of the dead and lay under a moonless sky, wondering about the next assault. Although he did not tell anyone, Howard doubted they could repel a massed charge by a determined enemy. From combat experience, he knew too that the enemy, having been badly mauled twice, would listen for sounds which would indicate his force had been shattered or demoralized before surging forward again.

Already up the slopes were floating the high, singsong taunts Marines had heard at other places in other wars. Voices which screeched: "Marines--you die tonight!" and "Marines, you die in an hour."

Members of the platoon wanted to return the compliments. "Sure," said Howard, "go ahead and yell anything you want." And the Marines shouted back down the slopes all the curses and invectives they could remember from their collective repetoire. The North Vietnamese screamed back, giving Howard the opportunity to deliver a master stroke in psychological oneupmanship.

"All right," he shouted. "Ready? Now!"

And all the Marines laughed and laughed and laughed at the enemy.

The North Vietnamese did not mount a third major attack and at 0100 an Air Force flare ship, with the poetic call sign of "Smoky Gold," came on station overhead. Howard talked to the pilot through his radio and the plane dropped its first flare. The mountainside was lit up. The Marines looked down the slopes. Lance Corporal Ralph Glober Victor stared, then muttered: "Oh my God, look at them." The others weren't sure it wasn't a prayer. North Vietnamese reinforcements filled the valley. Twenty-year-old Private First Class Joseph Kosoglow described it vividly: "There were so many, it was just like an ant hill ripped apart. They were all over the place."

They shouldn't have been. Circling above the mountain were attack jets and armed helicopters. With growing frustration, they had talked to Howard but could not dive to the attack without light. Now they had light.

They swarmed in. The jets first concentrated on the valley floor and the approaches to Nui Vu, loosing rockets which hissed down and blanketed large areas. Then those fast, dangerous helicopters--the Hueys--scoured the slopes. At altitudes as low as 20 feet, they skimmed the brush, firing their machine guns in long, sweeping bursts. The Hueys pulled off to spot for the jets, and again the planes dipped down, releasing bombs and napalm. Then the Hueys scurried back to pick off stragglers, survey the damage, and direct another run. One of the platoon's communicators, Corporal Martinez, said it in two sentences: "The Hueys were all over the place. The jets blocked the Viet Cong off."

Two Hueys stayed over Howard's position all night; when one helicopter had to return to home base and refuel, another would be sent out. The Huey pilots, Captain John M. Shields

and Captain James M. Perryman, Jr., performed dual roles--
they were the Tactical Air Controllers' Airborne (TACAs) who
directed the bomb runs of the jets and they themselves
strafed the enemy. The North Vietnamese tried unsuccessfully
to shoot the helicopters down and did hit two out of the four
Hueys alternating on station.

By the light of the flares, the jet pilots could see the
hill mass and distinguish prominent terrain features but
could not spot Howard's perimeter. To mark specific targets
for the jets, the TACAs directed "Smoky" to drop flares right
on the ground as signal lights and then called the jets down
to pulverize the spot. Howard identified his position by
flicking a re-filtered flashlight on and off, and, guiding
on that mark, the Huey pilots strafed within 25 meters of
the Marines.

Still on the perimeter itself the fight continued. In
the shifting light of the flares, the pilots were fearful of
hitting the Marines and had to leave some space unexposed
to fire in front of the Marines' lines. Into this space
crawled the North Vietnamese.

For the Marines it was a war of hide and seek. Having
run out of grenades, they had to rely on cunning and marksmanship to beat the attackers. Howard had passed the word to
fire only at an identified target--and then only one shot at
a time. The enemy fired all automatic weapons; the Marines
replied with single shots. The enemy hurled grenades; the
Marines threw back rocks.

It was a good tactic. A Marine would hear a noise and
toss a rock in that general direction. The North Vietnamese
would think it was a grenade falling and dive for another
position. The Marine would roll or crawl low to a spot from
which he could sight in on the position, and wait. In a few
seconds, the North Vietnamese would raise his head to see why
the grenade had not exploded. The Marine would fire one
round. The range was generally less than 30 feet.

The accuracy of this fire saved the life of Corpsman
Holmes. When he regained consciousness after a grenade had
knocked him out, he saw a North Vietnamese dragging away the
dead Marine beside him. Then another enemy reached over and
grasped him by the cartridge belt. The soldier tugged at him.

Lance Corporal Victor was lying on his stomach behind
a rock. He had been hit twice by grenades since the first
flare had gone off and could scarcely move. He saw an enemy
soldier bending over a fallen Marine. He sighted in and
fired. The man fell backward. He saw a second enemy tugging
at another Marine's body. He sighted in again and fired.

Shot between the eyes, the North Vietnamese slumped dead across Billie Holmes' chest. He pushed the body away and crawled back to the Marines' lines. His left arm was lanced with shrapnel, and his face was swollen and his head ringing from the concussion of the grenade. For the rest of the night, he crawled from position to position, bandaging and encouraging the wounded, and between times firing at the enemy.

Occasionally the flares would flicker out and the planes would have to break off contact to avoid crashing. In those instances, artillery under the control of the Special Forces and manned by Vietnamese gun crews would fill in the gap and punish any enemy force gathering at the base of Nui Vu.

"Stiff Balls," Howard had radioed the Special Forces camp at Hoi An, three miles south. "If you can keep Charlie from sending another company up here, I'll keep these guys out of my position."

"Roger, Carnival Time." Captain Louis Maris, of the Army Special Forces, had replied, using Howard's own peculiar call sign. Both sides kept their parts of the bargain and the South Vietnamese crews who manned the 105mm howitzers threw in concentration after concentration of accurate artillery shells.

"Howard was talking on the radio. He was cool," Captain John Blair, the Special Forces commanding officer, recalled afterwards. "He stayed calm all the way through that night. But," he chuckled, "he never did get our call sign right!"

In the periods of darkness, each Marine fought alone. How some of them died no one knows. But the relieving force hours later found one Marine lying propped up against a rock. In front of him lay a dead enemy soldier. The muzzles of their weapons were touching each others' chests. Two Marine entrenching tools were recovered near a group of mangled North Vietnamese; both shovels were covered with blood. One Marine was crumpled beneath a dead enemy. Beside him lay another Vietnamese. The Marine was bandaged around the chest and head. His hand still clasped the hilt of a knife buried in the back of the soldier on top of him.

At 0300, a flight of H34 helicopters whirled over Nui Vu and came in to extract the platoon. So intense was the fire they met that they were unable to land and Howard was told he would have to fight on until dawn. Shortly thereafter, a richochet struck Howard in the back. His voice over the radio faltered and died out. Those listening--the Special Forces personnel, the pilots, the high ranking officers of the 1st Marine Division at Chulai--all thought the end had come.

Then Howard's voice came back strong. Fearing the drowsing effect morphine can have, he refused to let Holmes administer the drug to ease the pain. Unable to use his legs, he pulled himself from hole to hole encouraging his men and directing their fire. Wherever he went, he dragged their lifeline--the radio.

Binns, the man whose shot had triggered the battle, was doing likewise. Despite severe wounds, he crawled around the perimeter, urging his men to conserve their ammunition, gathering enemy weapons and grenades for the Marines' use, giving assistance wherever needed.

None of the Marines kept track of the time. "I'll tell you this," said Howard, "you know that movie--The Longest Day? Well, compared to our night on the hill, The Longest Day was just a twinkle in the eye." But the longest night did pass and dawn came. Howard heralded its arrival. At 0525 he shouted, "O.K., you people, reveille goes in 35 minutes." At exactly 0600, his voice pealed out, "Reveille, reveille!" It was the start of another day and the perimeter had held.

On all sides of their position, the Marines saw enemy bodies and equipment. The North Vietnamese would normally have raked the battlefield clean but so deadly was the Marine fire that they left unclaimed many of those who fell close to the perimeter.

The firing had slacked off. Although badly mauled themselves, the enemy still had the Marines ringed in and did not intend to leave. Nor did haste make them foolhardy. They knew what the jets and the Hueys and the artillery and the Marine sharpshooting would do to them on the bare slopes in daylight. They slipped into holes and waited, intending to attack with more troops the next night.

Bursts of fire from light machine guns chipped the rocks above the Marines' heads. Firing uphill from concealed foxholes, the enemy could cut down any Marine who raised up and silhouetted himself against the skyline. Two of the .50 caliber machine guns were still firing sporadically.

There came a lull in the firing. A Huey buzzed low over the hillcrest, while another gunship hovered to one side, ready to pounce if the enemy took the bait. No one fired. The pilot, Major William J. Goodsell, decided to mark the position for a medical evacuation by helicopter. His Huey fluttered slowly down and hovered. Howard thought the maneuver too risky and said so. But Goodsell had run the risk and come in anyway. He dropped a smoke grenade. Still no fire. He waved to the relieved Howard and skimmed north over the forward slope, only 10 feet above the ground.

The noise of machine guns drowned out the sound of the helicopter's engines. Tracers flew toward the Huey from all directions. The helicopter rocked and veered sharply to the right and zigzagged down the mountain. The copilot, First Lieutenant Stephen Butler, grabbed the stick and brought the crippled helicopter under control, crash landing in a rice paddy several miles to the east. The pilots were picked up by their wingman. But Major Goodsell, who had commanded Squadron VMO-6 for less than one week, died of gunshot wounds before they reached the hospital.

The medical pickup helicopter did not hesitate. It came in. Frantically, Howard waved it off. He was not going to see another shot down. The pilots were dauntless but not invulnerable. The pilot saw Howard's signal and turned off, bullets clanging off the armor plating of the undercarriage. Howard would wait for the infantry.

In anger, the jets and the Hueys now attacked the enemy positions anew. Flying lower and lower, they crisscrossed the slopes, searching for the machine gun emplacements, offering themselves as targets, daring the enemy to shoot.

The enemy did. Another Huey was hit and crashed, its crew chief killed. The .50 calibers exposed their position and were silenced. Still the North Vietnamese held their ground. Perhaps the assault company, with all its automatic weapons and fresh young troops, had been ordered to wipe out the few Marines at any cost; perhaps the commanding officer had been killed and his subordinates were following dead orders; perhaps the enemy thought victory yet possible.

But then the Marine infantry came in. They had flown out at dawn but so intense was the enemy fire around Nui Vu, the helicopters had to circle for 45 minutes while jets and artillery blasted a secure landing zone. During that time, First Lieutenant Richard E. Moser, a H34 helicopter pilot, monitored Howard's frequency and later reported: "It was like something you'd read in a novel. His call sign was Carnival Time and he kept talking about these North Vietnamese down in holes in front of him. He'd say, 'you've gotta get this guy in the crater because he's hurting my boys.' He was really impressive. His whole concern was for his men."

On the southern slope of the mountain, helicopters finally dropped Charlie Company of the 5th Marines. The relief company climbed fast, ignoring sniper fire and wiping out small pockets of resistance. With the very first round they fired, the Marine 60mm mortar team knocked out the enemy mortar. Sergeant Frank Riojas, the weapons platoon commander, cut down a sniper at 500 yards with a tracer round from his M14. Marine machine gun sections were detached from the main

Men of C/1/5 start up Howard's Hill, as napalm burns on the slope. (Lt Freed's photo.)

Pinned down atop Howard's Hill, Lieutenant Philip Freed calls for air support. (Lt Freed's photo.)

body and sent up the steep fingers along the flanks of the hill to support by fire the company's movement. The North Vietnamese were now the hunted, as Marines scrambled around as well as up the slope, attempting to pinch off the enemy before they could flee.

The main column climbed straight upwards. While yet a quarter of a mile away, the point man saw recon's position on the plateau. The boulder which served as Howard's command post was the most prominent terrain feature on the peak. The platoon hurried forward. They had to step over enemy bodies to enter the perimeter. Howard's men had eight rounds of ammunition left.

"Get down," were Howard's first words of welcome. "There are snipers right in front of us." Another recon man shouted: "Hey, you got any cigarettes?" A cry went up along the line--not expressions of joy--but requests for cigarettes.

It was not that Howard's Marines were not glad to see other infantrymen; it was just that they had expected them. Staff Sergeant Richard Sullivan, who was with the first platoon to reach the recon Marines, said later: "One man told me he never expected to see the sun rise. But once it did, he knew we'd be coming."

The fight was not over. Before noon, in the hot daylight, despite artillery and planes firing in support, four more Marines would die.

At Howard's urging, Second Lieutenant Ronald Meyer quickly deployed his platoon along the crest. Meyer had graduated from the Naval Academy the previous June and intended to make the Marine Corps his career. He had spent a month with his bride before leaving for Vietnam. In the field he wore no shiny bars, and officers and men alike called him "Stump," because of his short, muscular physique.

Howard had assumed he was a corporal or a sergeant and was shouting orders to him. Respecting Howard's knowledge and performance, Meyer obeyed. He never did mention his rank. So Staff Sergeant Howard, waving off offers of aid, proceeded to direct the tactical maneuvers of the relieving company, determined to wipe out the small enemy band dug in not 20 meters downslope.

Meyer hollered for members of his platoon to pass him grenades. He would then lob them downslope toward the snipers' holes. By peering around the base of the boulder, Howard was able to direct his throws. "A little more to the right on the next one, buddy. About five yards farther. That's right. No, a little too strong." The grenades had little effect and the snipers kept firing. Meyer shouted he wanted air on the target. The word was passed back for the air liaison officer to come forward. The platoon waited.

Lance Corporal Terry Redic wanted to fire his rifle grenade at the snipers. A tested sharpshooter, he had several kills to his credit. In small fire fights he often disdained to duck, prefering to suppress hostile fire by his own rapid accurate shooting. Meyer's way seemed too slow. He raised up, knelt on one knee, and sighted downslope looking for a target. He never found one. The enemy shot first and killed him instantly.

Meyer swore vehemently. "Let's get that *****. You coming with me, Sotello?" "Yes, Stump." Lance Corporal David Sotello turned to get his rifle and some other men. Meyer didn't wait. He started forward with a grenade in each hand. "Keep your head down, buddy, they can shoot," yelled Howard.

Meyer crawled for several yards, then threw a grenade at a hole. It blasted an enemy soldier. He turned, looking upslope. Another sniper shot him in the back. Sotello heard the shot as he started to crawl down.

So did Hospitalman 3d Class John Markillie, the platoon corpsman. He crawled toward the fallen lieutenant. "For God's sake, keep your head down!" yelled Howard. Markillie reached his lieutenant. He sat up to examine the wound. A sniper shot him in the chest.

Another corpsman, Holloday, and a squad leader, Corporal Melville, crawled forward. They could not feel Meyer's pulse. Markillie was still breathing. Ignoring the sniper fire, they began dragging and pushing his body up the hill.

Melville was hit in the head. He rolled over. His helmet bounced off. He shook his head and continued to crawl. The round had gone in one side of the helmet and ripped out the other, just nicking the corporal above his left ear. Melville and Holloday dragged Markillie into the perimeter.

From Chulai, the battalion commander called his company commander, First Lieutenant Marshall "Buck" Darling. "Is the landing zone secure, Buck?" "Well," A pause. "...not spectacularly." Back at the base two noncommissioned officers were listening. "I wonder what he meant by that?" asked the junior sergeant. "What the hell do you think it means, stupid?" replied the older sergeant. "He's getting shot at."

Ignoring his own wounds, Corpsman Billie Holmes was busy supervising the corpsmen from Charlie Company as they administered to the wounded. With the fire fight still going on to the front, helicopter evacuation was not possible from within the perimeter. The wounded had to be taken rearward to the south slope. Holmes roved back and forth, making sure that all his buddies were accounted for and taken out.

The pilots had seen easier landing sites. "For the medical evacs," Moser said, "a pilot had to come in perpendicular to the ridge, then cock his bird around before he sat down. We could get both main mounts down--first--the--tail--well--sometimes we got it down. We were still taking fire."

Holmes reported that there was still one Marine, whom he had seen die, missing. Only after repeated assurances that they would not leave without the body were the infantry able to convince him and Howard that it was time they too left. They helped the Navy corpsman and the Marine sergeant to a waiting helicopter. Howard's job was done.

Another had yet to be finished. There was a dead Marine to be found somewhere on the field of battle. But before a search could be conducted, the last of the enemy force had to be destroyed.

First Lieutenant Phil Freed flopped down beside Melville. Freed was the forward air controller attached to Charlie Company that day. He had run the last quarter mile uphill when he heard Meyer needed air. With the rounds cracking near his head, he needed no briefing. He contacted two F8 Crusader jets circling overhead. "This is Cottage 14. Bring it on down on a dry run. This has to be real tight. Charley is dug in right on our lines." At the controls of the jets were First Lieutenants Richard W. Deilke and Edward H. Menzer.

"There were an awful lot of planes in the air," Menzer said. "We didn't think we'd be used so we called DASC (Direct Air Support Center) and asked for another mission. We got diverted to the FAC (Forward Air Controller), Cottage 14. He told us he had a machine gun nest right in front of him."

As they talked back and forth, Menzer thought he recognized Freed's voice. Later he learned he had indeed; Freed had flown jets with him in another squadron a year earlier.

Freed was lying in a pile of rocks on the military crest of the northern finger of the hill. Since he himself had flown the F8 Crusader, Freed could talk to the pilots in a language they understood. Still, he was not certain they could help. He didn't know whether they could come that close and still not hit the Marine infantrymen. On their first run, he deliberately called the jets in wide so he could judge the technical skills and precision of the pilots. Rock steady.

He called for them to attack in earnest. When they heard the target was 20 meters from the FAC, it was the pilots' turn to be worried. "As long as you're flying parallel to the people, it's O.K.," Menzer said. "Because it's a good shooting bird. But even so, I was leery at first to fire with troops that near."

Unknown to them, the two pilots were about to fly one of the closest direct air support missions in the history of fixed-wing aviation. They approached from the northeast with the sun behind them, and cut across the ridgeline parallel to the friendly lines. They strafed without room for error. The gunsight reflector plate in an F8 Crusader jet looks like a bullseye with the rings marked in successive 10-mil increments. When the pilots in turn aligned their sights while 3,000 feet away, the target lay within the 10-mil ring and the Marine position was at the edge of the ring. The slightest variance of the controls would rake the Marine infantrymen with fire. In that fashion, each pilot made four strafing passes, skimming by 10 to 20 feet above the ridge. Freed feared they would both crash, so close did their wings dip to the crest of the hill. The impact of the cannon shells showered the infantrymen with dirt. They swore they could tell the color of the pilot's eyes. In eight attacks, the jet pilots fired 350 20mm explosive shells into an area 60 meters long and 10 to 20 meters wide. The hillside was gouged and torn, as if a bulldozer had churned back and forth across it.

Freed cautiously lifted his head. A round cracked by. One enemy had survived. Somebody shouted that the shot came from the position of the sniper who had killed Meyer. The lieutenant's body lay several yards downslope.

The F8 Crusaders had ample fuel left. Menzer called to say they could make dummy runs over the position if the Marines thought it would be useful. Freed asked them to try it.

The company commander, Buck Darling, watched the jets. As they passed, he noticed the firing stopped momentarily. The planes would be his cover. "I'm going to get Stump. Coming, Brown?" he asked the nearest Marine.

Lance Corporal James Brown was not a billboard Marine. His offbeat sense of humor often conflicted with his superiors' sense of duty. His squad leader later recalled with a grimace one fire fight when the enemy caught the squad in a cross fire. The rounds were passing high over the Marines' heads. While everyone else was returning fire, Brown strolled over to a Vietnamese tombstone, propped himself against it with one finger, crossed his legs and yelled: "You couldn't hit me if I was buried here!" His squad leader almost did the job for the enemy.

On the hill relieving the recon unit, however, Brown was all business. He emptied several rifle magazines and hurled grenade after grenade. When he ran out of grenades, he threw rocks to keep the snipers ducking. All the while he screamed and cursed, shouting every insult and blasphemy he could think of. Howard had been very impressed, both with Brown's actions and with his vocabulary.

He was not out of words when Darling asked him to go after Meyer's body. As they crawled over the crest, Brown tugged at his company commander's boot. "Don't sweat it, Lieutenant, they can only kill us." Darling did not reply. They reached Meyer's body and tried to pull it back while crawling on their stomachs. They lacked the strength.

"All right, let's carry him." said Darling. It was Brown's turn to be speechless. He knew what had happened to every Marine on the slope who had raised his head--and here was his officer suggesting they stand straight up! "We'll time our moves with the jets." When the jets passed low, they stumbled and scrambled forward a few yards with their burden, then flattened out as the jets pulled up. The sniper snapped shots at them after every pass. Bullets chipped the rocks around them. They had less than 30 feet to climb. It took over a dozen rushes. When they rolled over the crest they were exhausted. Only the enemy was left on the slope.

The infantry went after him. Corporal Samuel Roth led his eight man squad around the left side of the slope. On the right, Sergeant Riojas set a machine gun up on the crest to cover the squad. A burst of automatic fire struck the tripod of the machine gun. A strange duel developed. The sniper would fire at the machine gun. His low position enabled him to aim in exactly on the gun. The Marines would duck until he fired, then reach up and loose a burst downhill, forcing the sniper to duck.

With the firing, the sniper could not hear the squad crashing through the brush on his right side. Roth brought his men on line facing toward the sniper. With fixed bayonets they began walking forward. They could see no movement in the clumps of grass and torn earth.

There was a lull in the firing. The sniper heard the squad, turned and fired. Bullets whipped by the Marines. Roth's helmet spun off. He fell. The other Marines flopped to the ground. Roth was uninjured. The steel helmet had saved a second Marine's life within an hour. He was not even aware that his helmet had been shot off. "When I give the word, kneel and fire," he said. "Now!" The Marines rose and their rounds kicked up dust and clumps of earth in front of them. They missed the sniper. He had ducked into his hole.

The Marines lay back down. Roth swore. "All right--put in fresh magazines and let's do it again." "Now!"

Just as the Marines rose, the sniper bobbed up like a duck in a shooting gallery. A bullet knocked him backwards against the side of his hole. Roth charged, the other Marines sprinting behind him. He drove forward with his bayonet. A grenade with the release pin intact rolled from the sniper's left hand. Roth jerked the blade back. The sniper slumped forward over his machine gun.

The hill was quiet. It was noon. Darling declared the objective secure. In the tall grass in front of Riojas' machine gun, the infantrymen found the body of the missing Marine. The Marines paused to search 39 enemy dead for documents, picked up 18 automatic weapons (most of them Chinese), climbed on board a flight of helicopters, and flew off the plateau.

The Marines lost 10 dead. Charley Company and the Huey Squadrons each lost two. Of the 18 Marines in the reconnaissance platoon, 6 were killed; the other 12 were wounded. Five members of Charlie Company were recommended for medals. Every Marine under Howard's command received the Purple Heart. Fifteen were recommended for the Silver Star; Binns and Holmes were nominated for the Navy Cross; Howard was recommended for the Medal of Honor.

If the action had centered around just one man, then it could be considered a unique incident of exceptional bravery on the part of an exceptional man. It is that. But perhaps it is something more. On June 14th, few would have noticed anything unique about the 1st Reconnaissance Platoon of Charley Company. Just in reading the names of its dead, one has the feeling that here are the typical and the average, who, well-trained and well-led, rose above normal expectations to perform an exemplary feat of arms: John Adams, Ignatius Carlisi, Thomas Glawe, James McKinney, Alcadio Mascarenas, Jerrald Thompson.

NO CIGAR

> Preface: The author accompanied the
> 3d Platoon, Company A, 5th Marines, on
> several long-range patrols during the period
> 16-24 June 1966. He took several pictures of the
> platoon while on the patrols, which were con-
> ducted along the outer fringe of the 1st
> Battalion's Tactical Area of Responsibility,
> approximately eight miles northwest of the
> Marine base at Chulai. This is the story
> of two consecutive patrols, typical of TAOR
> patrolling in what the Marines called the
> "war of the rice paddy farmers."

The patrol filed out through the battalion's defensive wire at 2030 on 23 June 1966. The assistant platoon leader and the guide from the company on the defensive perimeter counted each man. They checked figures: "48?"

"48."

"See you."

"Good luck. Remember we have a listening post out about 200 meters."

The platoon started across an area of small paddies and burnt underbrush. The column twisted and stumbled forward. There was no moon.

Whispers.

"Hold it up. Pass the word."

"What's wrong? Pass it back."

"One of Kohlbuss' men has sprained his ankle so bad he can't walk. Did it crossing the dike."

"Nuts. O.K. Tell him to go back to the wire himself," the platoon commander, First Lieutenant A. A. "Tony" Monroe said. "Have him crawl back if he has to. It's only a few yards. Bielecki, call battalion and tell them an injured Marine is coming back in. Don't shoot him."

Lieutenant Monroe signalled the point to move out again. They walked 20 yards. More whispering.

"Hold it up."

"Now what's the matter?"

"Mills has a toothache. It's killing him."

Staff Sergeant Albert Ellis, the platoon guide, walked up to the lieutenant.

"It's true, sir. You know he should have gone to the dentist last week. Three days out there now would really put a hurting on him."

"Great. Just great. Bielecki--call battalion and tell them not to shoot Mills either. He'll be coming in. Shall we leave before everybody goes back?"

The platoon moved forward. The point avoided the trails and stream beds. Across gullies, along the edges of the rice paddies, through whip-saw grass and scrub growth, the Marines trudged in single file.

An hour passed.

"Bielecki--tell battalion we've passed check point one."

Two hours. Three.

"Bielecki, tell them we've passed check point two."

The Marines twisted and wound their way toward an ambush site in the mountains seven miles to the west. The night was muggy and the Marines sweated freely. But it was not hot and little water was drunk.

The point came to a break in the undergrowth and the column stopped while scouts moved ahead. Having crossed a large rice paddy, they entered and searched a distant tree line. Finding the way clear, they waved the main body on. The platoon walked across this paddy, keeping well spread out even in the dark and moving rapidly. The undergrowth the platoon just left suddenly glowed with quick red lights which winked on and off. Three sharp explosions followed and the ground shook. The platoon sergeant, Staff Sergeant Berton Robinson, ran up from the tail end of the platoon.

"Sir, those dumb artillery people just missed us!"

"Glad to hear they did, Robbie." The Marines listening chuckled. "Let's get up that mountain before they try again. I told them we were coming out here tonight. They should have stopped those H&I /Harassing and Interdiction/ fires in our vicinity altogether."

The point started clambering up over rocks in a westerly

direction. Illumination flares burst silently a few miles to the south. The landscape was frozen in relief. A man watching from a foxhole could see in clear outline any moving figure. The Marines crouched down in the bushes and waited. The first parachute flares flickered out but fresh ones opened and swung gently downward. Whispers.

"Those damn Popular Forces are putting on their nightly show," growled one Marine. "The record is eight flares at one time. This show might top them all."

It did. The platoon commander waited patiently. Flares were expensive and not that plentiful. He was sure darkness would fall again soon.

The platoon was grateful for the break. They had been pushing steadily for four hours. The hill they faced was 195 meters high, its steepness indicated by contour intervals on the map which pressed against each other.

The flares did not cease. Monroe was amazed--and angered. He did not like the idea of climbing a hill when anyone at the top could see him coming. But he had no choice, if he wanted to reach the ambush site before dawn.

The Marines got to their feet. Corporal Charles Washington led his point squad ahead of the main body. The Marines used their hands, knees, and feet to climb. They traversed the slope back and forth, grasping for holds and pulling themselves upwards.

"I don't like this," the lieutenant whispered. "A few grenades would play hell with us. And we couldn't throw any; they'd bounce right back on our heads."

They reached the top. Monroe had his squads spread out. The Marines flopped down gasping. No one moved for many minutes. A few men threw up. Finally, Monroe called for his squad leaders and two staff sergeants. He outlined simply the plan they had discussed before leaving the battalion area: the platoon would split into two groups and set up separate ambush and reconnaissance sites on the north and south sides of Hill 176, a mile to the south. Monroe would take one group, with two squads and the artillery forward observer; Staff Sergeant Ellis would lead the second, with one squad and the 60mm mortar. They would communicate by radio.

Monroe motioned. It was time to saddle up, Washington's squad still in front, Ellis' group falling in at the rear. The last mile would be easy, since they could follow the ridgelines southwest until they arrived at Hill 176. Monroe planned to place his ambush along a trail where it crossed a low saddle; Ellis would climb the hill and set in on the other side. The

Marines walked against the skyline with unconcern. The ridge was steep and thick, preventing effective ambush from the flanks. The Marines to the front and rear treaded cautiously.

The subdued sound of static from the radio stopped, indicating that someone was trying to contact the platoon. So Private First Class William Bielecki, the platoon radioman, stopped to listen. "Roger. Out." "Sir, battalion says regiment was hit at 2400 by an estimated VC company and to look out. They're headed our way and might try to cross the saddle on 176 to get into the mountains."

Monroe checked his watch--0300.

"O. K. Pass the word. Make sure every man knows they're coming."

With the chances of an encounter high, the usual night sounds of a tired Marine patrol faded away. No canteen cups rattled, no one at the rear of the column coughed, no loose sling clattered against a rifle stock. The Marines climbed over the crest of a small rise and began walking downwards. The platoon was strung out in the saddle on the northern side of Hill 176. Small clumps of scrub growth dotted the slope.

It was 0400 when the point squad reached a deep gully, thick with secondary jungle growth. Through that tangle twisted a dry stream bed trail which led to the mountain to the west.

Voices.

Every Marine heard them: high pitched, distinct, near. The guerrillas were on the stream bed trail and jabbering freely--they were taking a break near the top of the trail. They were tired and, so close to the sanctuary of the mountains, not alert.

The Marines stopped but did not deploy. They waited for the platoon commander's decision. Monroe gambled. Hoping to catch the VC in a cross fire, he sent Washington's squad down to cross the trail and take the high ground on the other side.

Five minutes passed. Crack. Crack, Crack, Crack. In the gully, shots were exchanged. "Washington, get on that high ground," Monroe yelled. "Get out of there!"

Washington's men scrambled out of the gully on the far side.

"Fire a flare."

From the rear of the column a hand flare went up--in the wrong direction.

"No, stupid, down in the draw!"

Another flare popped. Forty Marines fanned out and peered down in the gully, shading their eyes against the glare of the flares still bursting to the south. On the far side eight more Marines did the same. The gully was filled with the weird flickering shadows of trees and bushes.

"There's one! Right across from us--up high--in front of Wash's people." The Marine fired his M14 three times. The figure disappeared.

Monroe was on the radio. "Enemy troops in draw. Request HE and illumination. Also request illumination at regiment be ceased immediately. It is lighting us up. Over."

Refused were the two requests concerning illumination. Approved was the request for a high explosive concentration. While Monroe was explaining his situation over the radio, Sergeants Robinson and Ellis swung the squads into a perimeter defense. Most weapons were pointed down toward the gully but a machine gun section climbed to the top of the hill and a fire team was sent out to listen to the rear. Washington's squad climbed to the peak of Hill 176 and set in there. The Marines could hear the VC, who had not returned fire, crashing through the bush below. Since there were no visible targets and Monroe did not want to expose his exact position and size, the Marines did not fire at the sounds. They waited for the artillery.

Forty minutes passed. The Marines could still hear noises, but only very faintly. The radio crackled. "On the way."
"Thanks a lot," Monroe answered sarcastically.

A sharp explosion was heard out in the rice paddies to the east of the hill.

"Left 100, drop 200. Fire three rounds."

Five minutes later the rounds smashed in.

"Drop 50, fire for effect." Two minutes later the hill shook. The Marines lay low as fragments hummed in flight up the hillside. Robinson yelled at the lieutenant over the noise: "That's right down there!"

"Yes--but they're long gone by now." Monroe replied.

Silence.

"All right--everyone lie still and listen," Monroe shouted.

A Marine on the forward listening post shouted back:

"I can hear them splashing through the paddies, sir. They're making a hat*."

"Left 200, add 400, fire for effect."

Three minutes later the shells landed.

"Right in there. Cannot survey results. Thank you. Out."

It was getting light. Ellis gathered his group and set out for the far side of the hill. Washington stayed in position, while Monroe put his men in the draw along the trail to shield them from the coming sun. He doubted if anyone else would use the trail during the day.

With two radio operators, his platoon sergeant, and the artillery forward observer, Monroe crawled into the bushes above the trail to observe the scattered hamlets to the east. At dawn, he scanned with binoculars the flat lands below him. "There they are, just like last time," he said. In a grove of trees a half-mile away, two figures stood close together. Both were wearing dark green uniforms and carrying rifles.

"When you try to get close to that village, they fire three warning shots and make it," Robinson explained to the forward observer.

Monroe was busy plotting coordinates. The forward observer did the same--they compared the results, then called for a fire mission and requested a volley of six rounds without adjustment.

The rounds crashed into the trees. One figure fell. The other disappeared from sight. The Marines at the observation post exchanged grins.

The sun rose high and bare and the heat beat down, smothering. By noon not even an insect flew to inspect or bite the sweating Marines. Each man had left base camp with three full canteens. Most had drunk two, the third had to last until the next day. The Marines sat and watched. They talked and moved little.

Occasionally they saw the Viet Cong. Some were carrying weapons, some wore packs, some were dressed in black peasant shirts and shorts, some in green uniforms. They travelled freely in small groups of from two to eight men. They crossed the rice paddies, chatted with the women hoeing or the boys herding cows, and entered various hamlets, without any apparent military pattern or plan to their movements. The enemy seemed unaware that the shells which fell sporadically near them were observed fire missions, although some were hit and dragged away.

---

*make a hat - Marine slang for attempting to escape; moving away quickly

Lieutenant "Tony" Monroe, platoon leader of A/1/5, pauses while calling in a fire mission against the VC. (Author's)

Corporal Charles Washington stands in front of the bushes where the VC crawled away from Sergeant Ellis' men. (Author's)

A 105mm howitzer of the 11th Marines emplaced in its aiming circle during operations in June 1966. (USMC A369187)

Monroe requested that a Marine company sweep the area. From his observation post, he could direct their movements. Charlie Company arrived by foot two hours later and the platoons spread out on line to sweep the hamlets.

A quarter of a mile in front of the company, Robinson saw a group of armed VC in uniforms run across a rice paddy and enter a large house. They reappeared moments later, wearing black pajamas, straw conical hats, and carrying hoes. They split up and waded into the rice paddies.

"Look at them--the innocent farmers. They're going to get the surprise of their lives when they're scoffed up--hoes and all--in a few minutes," Monroe said.

It was Monroe who was surprised; the company was ordered back to base camp to perform another mission.

"We'll get that hooch* ourselves on our way in tomorrow morning," he said.

The platoon passed a quiet night. After the action of the night before, no one walked up the draw. The Marines rested--and thought of water. It was a night of stars, cool and without many mosquitos. A few miles to the northeast Bravo Company, heavily engaged with a VC company, called for 155mm artillery support. Monroe's platoon listened to the situation reports over the radio and watched the bright, quick flashes of the big shells as they smashed in.

"Just like watching a war flic at a drive-in movie back home," quipped one Marine.

"Yeh," replied his buddy. "Pass me the buttered popcorn, sweetie."

At dawn, the Marines left their ambush positions and filed down the trail. Monroe left Ellis on the high ground with a machine gun team and a radio to cover the platoon and alert them of enemy movements. The Marines skirted the rice paddies, staying in the tree lines and heading for the house where the VC had changed clothes the day before. They passed a pool of water and slowed down, each man pausing to dunk one canteen, watchful lest a leech swim into the open top. They passed a dozen men and women working in a rice paddy. The Vietnamese ignored them.

Ellis' voice came over the radio. "You're being followed. Two men with weapons are in the brush behind your rear man."

"Fudge and Baily--drop off and zap the guys coming up behind us," Monroe said.

---
*hooch - Marine slang for native house

The two Marines had scarcely turned around when Ellis' machine gun fired a burst, then another. Again his voice came over the radio. "They were closing on your right flank. Watch it. The people who were working in the paddy are making it."

"Corporal Figgins--move your squad out into the paddy to our right. Stop those people trying to get away. Don't shoot if you can help it--just grab them."

The Marines broke from the tree line at a dead run. The 2d Squad and mortar crew set up along the tree line in support.

Three Vietnamese were in the field.

"Halt. Halt. Damn it--halt!" Lance Corporal George Armstrong yelled.

The Vietnamese split up and ran faster.

Two ran east directly towards the house the platoon intended to search with several Marines in close pursuit. One Vietnamese stumbled and fell. The other turned to help. They were caught.

One turned to the west. He ran swiftly and the angle of his flight put him farther and farther from the Marines. A rifleman stepped up on a rice paddy dike and snapped two warning shots high in the air. The figure ran even faster. The rifleman dropped to his right knee, placed his left elbow on his left knee, and fitted his cheek along the stock of his rifle. His movements were deliberate, not hurried. He fired once. The figure fell.

The lieutenant led the 2d Squad forward and set them in near the VC house. The corpsman trotted past the rifleman.

"Take your time, doc. I shot him in the leg."

A helicopter evacuation was called and the wounded Vietnamese flown to a hospital. The two other fugitives were women, indistinguishable from men at a distance. They were sullen and stolid and ignored their Marine captors.

The Marines searched the VC house, a two-room dwelling made of thatch and bamboo. It was empty, as they had expected it to be after the firing started. A squad split into fire teams and prodded the thickets near the house.

"Here's an entrance to one tunnel in this briar patch."

"Here's another near the gate

"Don't touch that gate or the fence. It may be booby-trapped."

"Hey, Corporal Figgins, I'm no boot. I'm walking all the way around, see?"

"O. K. big mouth, let's see how loud you can shout for somebody to come out."

In Vietnamese, the Marine hollered several times and kicked dirt into the tunnel opening.

"Nothing. I don't hear nothing. And it sure as hell isn't a family bomb bunker."

"Right. Blow them both. And get back in case there's a secondary explosion."

"Hey, corporal, how many times do I have to tell you I'm no ----."

"Shut up and get to work. Milton, you check for other entrances."

"Fire in the hole!"* The muffled explosions of grenades followed the shout.

The Marines waited for the smoke to clear, then explored the tunnels, finding only a paper Viet Cong flag and a bag of cement mix. They burned the house. The women began to cry, having finally realized the Marines did not come on a random search. They knew they were suspect and would be taken in for questioning.

The Marines ignored their tears. If the women had not run across the open rice paddies, they might have taken the VC men by surprise. They were hot, and sweaty, and tired. They had wounded or killed several VC by artillery, but only one by small arms fire. That fact irritated them. They spread out and trudged back to base camp. They would try again the next day.

* * * * * * * * * *

The platoon rested that afternoon. The next day the men cleaned their equipment, drank beer, sang songs, dozed on their cots in the hot canvas squad tents, and waited for nightfall.

At 1800 on 26 June, they blackened their faces, rechecked their ammunition, and replotted compass courses on the maps. At 1900, Monroe inspected them and went over a final time with the squad leaders the route, length, and mission of the patrol

---

*"Fire in the hole" - Marine slang for warning of an impending explosion

"O. K. We're the ambush slash observation slash blocking force for the sweep tomorrow morning. How's that for a combo? The last time out it took eight hours to get to that damn saddle. This hump out will last even longer. Any questions?"

There were none. They were an old platoon, used to each other and to the war, secretly proud of their ability to make long, silent night marches. Within the battalion they were known as "Monroe's Nightcrawlers." They thought the nickname was appropriate.

At 2000, the platoon approached the battalion's defensive wire. The guide called softly to Lieutenant Monroe.

"How many?"

"38."

"O. K. Follow me."

"No."

"Huh?"

"You heard me. I'm not going to parade my people over that skyline just before I leave the position. Go around the shoulder of the hill."

"Oh, sure, right."

The platoon started forward. A few hours earlier, it had rained, a short, thick torrent. The damp ground and sopping bushes muffled the sounds of the passing men. Someone belched loudly as they cleared the wire. Robinson groaned. Monroe just shook his head.

The footing was treacherous and the cleats on the jungle boots clogged with mud. After walking for 40 minutes, the point man waded across a swollen stream and slipped twice scrambling up the far bank. The bank became more slippery with the passage of every man. The crossing proved costly. Two Marines near the end of the column twisted their ankles.

"Damn," hissed Monroe. "From now on I'm going to have all men with weak ankles tape them before night patrols. This happens every time out."

"Sergeant Robinson, take a man from each squad and stay here with them. Keep your radio on all night but don't speak unless it's an emergency. Fire the red flare if you get in trouble. In the brush with your backs to the paddy, you've got a good defensive position and I don't think you'll be spotted. I'll have a med evac pick you up in the morning. See you."

"Sure, sir. Good hunting."

The point Marine avoided the trails and hamlets, setting a course through scrub brush and around rice paddies. At the edge of one open field, he heard a snorting noise. Lying down, he bobbed his head back and forth like a boxer, trying to silhouette some object against the skyline. He succeeded and whispered: "Water buffalos. Watch yourselves."

The Marines cautiously filed around the side of the field opposite the powerful, horned animals, taking care not to disturb them, lest they charge.

The undergrowth became thicker, reaching shoulder height. Near the middle of the column there was a sudden thrashing in the bushes. The Marines stopped. The bushes danced wildly as some swift animal wheeled back and forth beside the still column. A low growl was heard, followed by a short burst from an automatic rifle.

A Marine spoke, lowly but distinctly. "No, no, no, you clown. If that was a tiger, he was just trying to make it."

Since his position had been compromised, Monroe changed the patrol route and the point set off at a fast pace in another direction. The platoon followed. The brush thickened into heavy secondary jungle growth. Those who thought to bring them put on gloves, since many trees and vines were covered with thorns. The leaves and thickets cut off all light from the sky, and so dark was it that it made no diffeence whether the Marines opened or shut their eyes. The interval between men closed completely. The vines and thorns formed solid fences and forced the men to grope for any small openings. Often they crawled on their hands and knees. Sometimes they doubled back or cut at right angles to their compass heading. In one hour they moved 200 yards.

When they did emerge from the jungle they were faced by a river. The point squad fanned out up and down stream to find a fording place. Finding such a spot, a fire team waded through the neck-deep water and entered the tree line on the other side. Ten minutes later, one Marine waded back across and spoke to the lieutenant. "Clear." Two men at a time, the platoon crossed.

At 0500, the platoon arrived at the objective. Monroe sent one squad with Ellis to a hill overlooking the flat land to the north. He set the rest of the platoon in an L-shaped ambush along the main trail leading from the village which was to be searched at 0600 by Bravo and Charlie Companies.

By 0545, it was light enough to recognize a man at 20 meters. The platoon moved north down the trail. Monroe had orders to proceed to a hill selected by map reconnaissance. He radioed back that the hill provided no observation of the village and requested permission to move forward to a better vantage point. Permission was granted.

Ten minutes later, while the platoon was still on the move, a jet screamed in from the south and passed low over the selected landing zone, an open rice paddy 400 meters northeast of the village. As the Marines watched, the bright orange of napalm was splashed against the red dawn. In common fascination, the entire column halted and stared. "Almost makes you forget you're fighting a war," murmured one Marine.

"Sir, there they are!"

A half a mile away to the Marines' left front, a group of 30 Vietnamese was crossing a rice paddy.

"Are they carrying weapons?" The binoculars were uncased. "There's not enough light to see, sir. But they have kids walking on their flanks."

The Marines just looked at each other. They were reasonably sure it was a band of fleeing Viet Cong. But they were not positive. And there were children.

In a few minutes, the band would be on the other side of a hill to the Marines' left.

"Nuts. Let's get up that hill and scope them out."

"Sir, there are two more--on the hill."

Peering down over the tops of the bushes were two Vietnamese. The Marines could see no weapons.

"Should we cut them down?"

"No--it might be just some scared farmer--though I doubt it. Figgins--get your squad up that hill on the double."

The Vietnamese ducked from view. Forming a skirmish line, the squad raced up the hill and peered down into the draw on the other side.

"There they go--three of them, around the side of the next hill. One of them is carrying a rifle."

The squad leader estimated the range at 600 yards. The Marines adjusted their sights, knelt down, and began firing.

"Hold them and squeeze them--hold them and squeeze them. At that range you're not going to hit nothing if you just crank them off."

Corporal Bierwirth brought up his squad. He adjusted the sights on his stubby M79 grenade launcher, pointed the muzzle high, and fired. A burst of smoke appeared in front of one of the Viet Cong and the man fell. His two companions ducked into the brush.

Lieutenant Monroe checked the terrain. "Bierwirth--you stay here. Figgins--your squad comes with me up the next hill. That band might be hiding on the other side. Bielecki--tell Ellis to come down the trail."

The lieutenant left and Bierwirth put lookouts on each side of the hill.

"Corporal--one of them's circled behind us and is hitting it across the paddy."

The squad leader called for two riflemen. The fleeing Viet Cong could be seen clearly through binoculars, 1,000 years away. The riflemen raised their sights as high as they could and sat down where they could see over the brush. They began firing, every fifth round a tracer. The Marine with the binoculars watched the strike of the bullets and called corrections.

The Viet Cong zigzagged, running as fast as he could. A bullet struck him and he went down. Then he regained his feet and staggered off. He was not hit again.

"Probably only grazed him. Lucky to do that at that distance," said one Marine.

Another lookout ran up to Bierwirth.

"They're behind us--where we just came from. A whole squad of 'em."

"Sure it's not Sergeant Ellis' squad?"

"Naw--they're too well camouflaged to be Marines."

Bierwirth looked down through the binoculars. On the trail heading south he saw a line of figures in Khaki uniforms, covered with leaves and braches. In the lead was a Viet Cong dressed in black peasant garb and wearing a straw hat. All were carrying weapons.

As Bierwirth watched, they ducked into the bushes. "Must have seen Ellis coming. Quick, slam them with a LAAW and get that gun working."

A machine gunner started firing from the hip. The bullets sprayed the area. "No. Get down and use it."

"I can't see down there."

"Clear a field of fire and use your tripod."

"I don't have no machete or entrenching tool. And we didn't bring the pod."

"They're gonna make it if Ellis doesn't nail them. Fire that damn LAAW."

The high explosive shell burst short of the brush.

"Missed. But Ellis will know where they are."

The Marines heard a slight swishing sound above their heads. Three pounding flashes erupted on the hill behind them.

"God! The lieutenant!"

Fifty meters to the right of the artillery bursts, a group of Marines jumped out of the brush and waved their arms frantically. Monroe was roaring into the radio, his voice carrying distinctly to Bierwirth's hill. The Marines laughed nervously with relief.

"Boy, is he giving them hell. It'll be a long time before that artillery observer shoots at an unidentified target again."

Sergeant Ellis came up the trail. Over the radio Monroe directed him to fire into the brush to his right and then search it for the enemy squad. Ellis did so, but his men found only trails of flattened grass; the Viet Cong had slipped away in the confusion which followed the misdirected artillery fire.

A fire team moved down the draw to recover the body of the VC Bierwirth killed with his grenade launcher. The body was gone.

Another fire team checked the trail the first large group of Vietnamese followed. It was plainly marked every ten or twenty meters by three stones set like triangles with the point toward the trail--Viet Cong markings for an unmined path.

Monroe gathered his force and reluctantly headed back to the base camp. As they walked tiredly along, two Marines looked at each other.

"Next time," one said.

"Yeh--next time."

NOTE: The next time did come for the 3d Platoon, and on 10 August 1966, they distinguished themselves in a pitched battle described in the last chapter of this narrative.

NIGHT ACTION

Preface: The author spent 10 days with these Marines from Charlie Company, 7th Marines, who were training and fighting with some Vietnamese militia in the village of Binh Yen No (1), about seven miles southwest of the 1st Marine Division Headquarters at Chulai. In addition to participating in the patrols as an extra rifleman, he taped a few of the actual ambushes, as well as the comments of the men concerning their combined action work.

This is not one story. It is a diary relating several night patrols. The participants are 13 Marines, numerous Vietnamese villagers and militia, and Viet Cong. The Marines lived with and trained the Popular Forces (PF), a few dozen local farmers who had agreed with the central government to protect their village in return for exemption from draft into the regular army. The Marines had volunteered for the job because it promised action and an escape from company routine. They found the action.

In one week, from 7-13 July 1966, the 13 Marines killed 31 guerrillas. They set 16 ambushes and made contact 9 times. On three occasions, the VC ambushed the Marines; each time the Marines seized the offensive within a few minutes, forcing the VC to break contact. In many engagements the Marines were outnumbered; but fire discipline, shooting accuracy, and aggressiveness compensated for numbers.

The ultimate goal of the Marines was to train and develop the PF forces so that the Marines would no longer be needed to protect the village. The men did not deceive themselves; they knew that goal would not be reached in a few short months. And until the PFs were a competent fighting force, the Marines would carry the main burden of combat around the village.

This is an attempt to describe how the Marines and PF operated.

13 July 1966. Six Marines assembled in the small courtyard of the Popular Forces fort. The squad leader, Sergeant Joseph Sullivan, wore jungle utilities and a Marine utility cover. He carried an M14 automatic, seven magazines, two green star cluster flares, one red star cluster, and a flashlight. The uniforms of the other were less according to regulation. One wore a Swiss alpine hat, another a beret, a third was clad in black utilities, a fourth Marine wore no cover. Three

carried M14 automatics; the fourth an M79 grenade launcher. Each had a LAAW slung across his shoulder. The radio operator also carried an M14 automatic and had a PRC-10 strapped to his back.

Two PFs joined the patrol after Sullivan had inspected his men. They were dressed in green utilities and bush hats. One carried a carbine, the other a Thompson submachine gun. One was placed at the point of the column, the other a few men back. (It was the belief of the Marines at that time that the PFs could spot a VC in that locale at night before a Marine could. They subsequently changed their minds.)

Few words were exchanged. Nothing was new to the Marines about the patrol. They knew the area and the mission well; go down to the river and ambush the VCs who tried to cross. G-2 had warned that day that a hard-core battalion was operating in the vicinity. The news was accepted skeptically. There were so many warnings from so many sources received each day.

After curfew, the patrol filed out of the fort, passing across a stagnant moat studded with bamboo stakes and through a tall bamboo fence designed to stop grenades. In theory, recoilless rifle shells would also explode against it and not against the long sand-plaster building in the fort.

The PF at point turned left and walked a hundred meters to an outer fence. Three unarmed villagers, serving as gate-openers and sentries, looked at them blankly for a moment. Then one noisily pushed open the gate; another lifted a wooden mallet and began tapping against a bamboo pole, tap..tap..tap ..tap..tap..tap..tap. Supposedly this was the villagers' signal that the VC were on the prowl. The Marines looked at each other uneasily. They didn't like having their exit announced, but the PFs seemed unbothered.

In column they moved east across the rice paddies and entered the main street of Binh Yen No (1). The street was a straight, narrow dirt path leading northeast, overshadowed by palm trees and thick brush and lined with thatched huts. Although it was not yet 2030, the street was pitch dark. Only by shifting glances and looking at various angles could each Marine distinguish the outline of the man in front of him. The villagers were still awake and the Marines heard chatter from many houses. Lights shone from some doorways and fell across the street. The Marines hurried across these lighted patches.

The villagers knew a patrol was passing. Some warned the VC by signals. In one house a man coughed loudly and falsely. Farther on, an old lady shifted her lantern from one room to another as the Marines slipped by.

The patrol reached the far end of the town without drawing fire and left the tree line. For a quarter of a mile, they followed the dikes between open rice paddies, then they turned right and walked about fifty meters to the river. The bank was sprinkled with skimpy shrubbery and carpeted with human waste. The Marines called the ambush site "The Head." It provided excellent fields of fire over the river, but it took a strong man to withstand the smell.

The Marines lay down and slowly took off their cartridge belts and placed them beside their weapons. The bipods for the M14s were extended gently. There was no wind and a slight sound would carry to the opposite bank.

At each end of the line a Marine was stationed to watch the rear and outboard flanks. The river was 100 meters wide at the ambush point. Many nights the VC came down the river to get supplies and visit their families who lived in Binh Yen No (1). Sometimes they paddled downstream in small boats; sometimes they crept along the far bank and waded across at fording points.

The Marines settled down to wait. Droves of mosquitoes descended on the men. They didn't dare slap them away. A few unfortunates disturbed some red ants. They crept to other positions, cursing under their breaths and praying the ambush would be soon sprung.

The Viet Cong tried to accommodate the wish. No sooner were the Marines in position and being bitten than firing broke out to their right, coming from the village. Red tracers streaked high over the Marines' heads. Sergeant Sullivan identified the weapons. "Automatic carbine. Two Russian blowbacks, maybe M1s. Lie still. Don't return fire. They're trying to get us to give away our position," he whispered. The VC fired three bursts in the general direction of the patrol, then stopped.

One hour passed. The Marines heard a few splashes near the far bank but saw no movement. A second hour went by. More scattered probing fire came from the VC. Sullivan suspected the patrol might have passed an enemy outpost, which was now trying to locate the Marine position so their main force could avoid it. The sergeant whispered to his men to be still. They would play a waiting game and force the VCs to move first.

During the next hour, the Marines heard a few splashes down river and saw a dull light bobbing along the far bank. It appeared that the VC were portaging supplies inland after crossing farther down river.

By midnight, when the patrol still had not fired, the enemy lost caution and started to move freely. Frequent

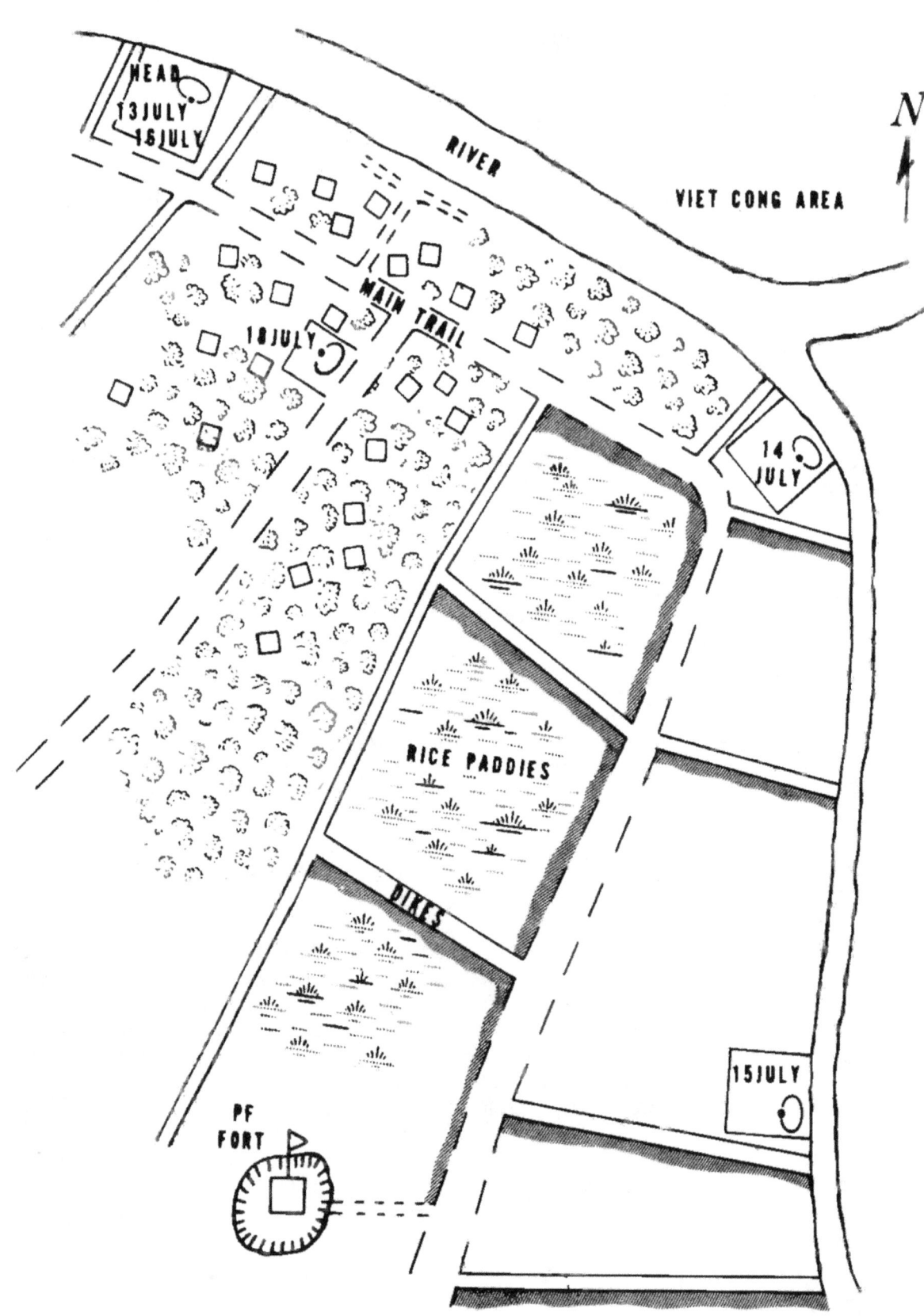

SCHEMATIC SKETCH TO ACCOMPANY "NIGHT ACTION"

splashes and the mutter of low voices carried clearly to the Marines. There came the distinct clank of a heavy bundle striking the bottom of a boat.

Corporal Leland Riley, who had the eyes of a hawk, whispered, "I see them. Two-three boats...and a bunch of them on the bank--right across from us."

"Yeh, LAAWs up."

Two Marines slowly extended two rocket tubes.

"See them?"

"No. Wait. Now I do."

"Fire when ready."

The sharp explosions of the recoilless weapons rang the ears of all the Marines. Momentarily deaf, they could not even hear the blasts from their own automatic weapons. But the six Marines were blazing away, holding down their rifles, the bipods enabling them to keep their bursts low. With every other round in the magazines a tracer, they placed their shot groups where they thought they saw or heard the enemy. Hundreds of bullets skimmed across the river and swept the opposite bank.

Water splashed some Marines in the face. "What the hell?" yelled Private First Class Kenneth Lerch. "Hey, we're getting some incoming." The fire fight was 15 seconds old.

"Cease fire! Shut up and listen up," Sullivan shouted.

Silence. A few seconds went by. Then a distinct splashing was heard near the other bank. Someone was wading out of the water, trying to climb the bank.

Two Marines fired, their tracers converged, then swept back and forth. Again there was silence. It was anybody's guess whether they had hit the enemy or if he were just standing still in the water, waiting until the Marines went away.

Next there came through the air a sound like someone ripping paper, followed by a loud pop. An 81mm mortar flare burst over the river, and began its squeaking, dangling descent beneath its small parachute.

The illumination had been provided in accordance with a preplanned system. When the LAAWs went off, the Marine radio watch back at the fort heard and took a compass bearing on the noise. There were three patrols out but each had gone in a widely different direction, so the Marine could easily identify the patrol. He called the command post at Charlie Company and said simply, "Andy Capp 68," thus identifying the patrol by a prearranged code. From the C.P. the word was shouted to the stand-by mortar crew lounging 50 feet away.

"81s--illum--68."

Sergeant Martin, the mortar section leader, had preplotted the firing data for the ambush sites of all the night patrols. He checked his card for #68 and called:

"Deflection--2650. Elevation--0800. Charge 6. Fire when up." Less than 10 seconds after the call reached Charlie Company the first of three illumination rounds was on its way.

Under its glare, the Marines could see the other river bank clearly. Nothing was moving. The tall sawgrass was still.

"Check those boats," Riley said.

Pulled up on the bank were two dark, canoelike shapes.

"Check them, hell. Blast them," Sullivan replied.

The other two LAAWs were quickly opened and fired. The first hit to the left but the second one exploded dead on. Short bursts from the automatic rifles further splintered the hulls.

The last flare died out. It was 20 minutes past midnight.

"We put a hurting on some of them," an anonymous voice said.

"Maybe tomorrow night we can catch them on our side of the river. Let's head back in," Sullivan said.

During the next day, the villagers brought news to the fort that one of the patrols the night before had fired upon a VC company who had come north on a resupply mission. The villagers--and the PFs--thought the Marines were slightly crazy to open fire on a VC force of unknown size. The Marines were disappointed. They would have called in a priority artillery mission if they had known there were so many Viet Cong.

<u>14 July 1966</u>. The patrols left the fort at 2000. It was just dark.

"We're gonna get some more tonight," Private First Class Lerch yelled to the PFs and village chiefs who were milling around inside the fort.

The same patrol returned to the river. They set in near a group of bamboo fish traps, a mile downstream from "The Head."

Three kerosene lights marked a channel through the traps. Night lights on the river were officially forbidden since they served as beacons for the VC. But some stubborn fishermen ignored the order night after night. The Marines, as advisors, could not make the PFs enforce the order.

The patrol hid behind some dirt mounds along the bank and waited. To go down river, the VCs would have to pass through the fishermens' channels. The enemy were not long in coming.

The disturbed squawkings of ducks and geese alerted the patrol. The VC were paddling down river. It was next to impossible to pass a raft of waterfowl at night without scaring them up. The VCs, however, would sometimes tie geese to their boats and try to pass as a raft of birds, hoping the Marines would fire behind them.

A light shone through a clump of bushes on the far bank. The Marines heard the dull sound of wood scraping against wood.

"They're carrying a boat over the fish traps," Sullivan whispered.

Corporal Riley, ignoring the activity on the river, had been watching to the rear. "There's someone moving in on our right flank," he whispered.

Riley and another Marine moved down the bank to prevent an enemy probe. Lance Corporal Gerald Faircloth, the squad's best shot with a LAAW, heard paddle splashes near the fish traps. "I think I can hit that next boat when they climb the traps," he whispered.

"O. K., blast them," Sullivan replied.

Faircloth knelt on his left knee. He placed the short fiberglass tube on his right shoulder. The tube wavered up and down, then steadied. Flame spurted from both ends. One hundred yards away there was a bright flash. The Marines started sweeping the river with automatic rifle fire. Riley emptied a magazine into the bushes along the bank to his right.

Overhead, a mortar flare blossomed. "There they are!" Riley shouted.

The firing caught two Viet Cong in a round wicker basket boat trying to cross the river behind the fish traps. In the sudden light they were easy targets. They dove overboard just as Riley and another Marine opened fire. The tracers ripped through the boat and whipped the water. Standing on the bank the two Marines changed magazines and waited to see if the head of either Viet Cong resurfaced. They did not. The light boat rocked to and fro. The surface of the river was calm and shone brightly under the fire.

"I guess that's that," Riley said.

The other Marine didn't have a chance to reply. Bullets hummed between them. Both were diving off the bank before they heard the sound of the machine gun. They sprawled behind the rice paddy dike. Without lifting his head, Riley yelled, "It's coming from the other side. They've got us spotted. Get them off us."

To the Marines crouching 50 yards away, the acrobatics had provided an interesting spectacle. Their main position had not been seen by the Viet Cong and they were not under fire. They took their time and did not expose their position by chancing a random burst of small arms fire at the machine gun.

Faircloth extended another LAAW. He gauged the distance at 100 yards. The light was good. Faircloth had hit point targets at 300 yards. He sighted in, then paused.

"So that's what they were doing in those bushes with a light. Setting up a gun to cover them," Lance Corporal Sidney Fleming said, as if discussing a subject of purely academic interest.

"Come on, come on. You just stay put, Riley," yelled Sullivan.

"Oh God, I don't believe it," groaned Riley.

Faircloth fired. The explosion was muffled by the bushes. Faircloth had hit his target. The chatter of the machine gun stopped.

"You two dingers can come home now," laughed Sullivan.

The two Marines returned from the flank. They did not walk on the dike; crouching low beside it, they trotted back. The Marines formed a hasty circular perimeter, lay down and waited. The last flare hissed out. The Marines did not talk or move. They were waiting to trap any infiltrator who might have crept close during the firing. For 10 minutes they lay perfectly still, listening to the night sounds and trying to detect any sharp change of tempo in the croaks of the frogs and crickets or the surprised squawks of waterfowl. They listened for feet to crush in the bush or slurp in the mud. They could detect no human movement.

Sullivan broke the silence with a whisper.

"Pack it in. Keep it spread,"

Popular Forces militiaman, armed with a carbine and portable radio, moves toward the main gate in bamboo fence surrounding the PF fort at Binh Yen No (1). (Author's photo)

Sergeant Joseph Sullivan, leader of the Marine patrols operating near Binh Yen No (1), stands on the river bank; beyond him is VC territory. (Author's photo.)

15 July 1966. That night a different Marine patrol went to a different point on the river. It was to be a short patrol, travelling not more than 400 meters away from the fort. At night the Viet Cong sneaked around all sides of the fort to enter the village where their families lived. Some drifted down the river right in front of the fort, having observed that the Marines roved far and wide and left the short patrols mostly to the PFs. So Corporal Franklin Lummis led out a security force at 2000 to seek the enemy close-in.

The four Marines and two PFs crossed a series of five rice paddies to reach the river bank, walking on the dike walls without cover or concealment. If fired upon from the river bank, they would drop behind a dike. Each mud dike is a few feet high and over a foot thick. A 106mm recoilless rifle on a nearby hill covered the area and could pulverize the river bank, if called upon.

Without incident the patrol reached the river bank, which had been built up to prevent the waters from flooding the paddies at high tide. The river bed itself was bordered by thick clumps of mangroves. Water buffalo came to the river to soak, and through the years their heavy passage had cut a 20-foot swath in the brush. From this inlet the main stream could be seen 15 meters away. A sandbar jutted up 20 meters farther out in the river.

Lummis led his patrol over the dike and into the dark hollow of the inlet. He was worried about infiltrators and so he set two Marines out to guard the right flank. Another Marine and a PF watched the dike and the mangroves to the left. Lummis kept Lance Corporal Joseph Bettie and the other PF with him. The three sat in the inlet.

On the right, Lance Corporal Phillip Brannon crawled onto the dike and lay behind a large bush. His automatic weapon pointed down the dike as he watched the skyline. Suddenly, his body tautened and he leaned forward, his cheek resting against the rifle stock. At the edge of the mangroves below the dike another Marine sat motionless, listening for a careless foot in the swamp and watching Brannon. He saw Brannon slowly slip off his safety. He unwound the elastic from the spoon of a grenade and pulled the bent-back edges of the holding pin straight. Brannon had seen a figure creeping up the dike, but it disappeared into the black swamps. Brannon relaxed slightly and jerked his head in the direction of the swamp. The Marine with the grenade strained to listen, and thought he heard a faint rustle of bushes. But not being sure it was a man, he did not throw his grenade. Instead, he sat poised for action and utterly still.

On the river ducks and geese started squawking, then the racket died down. But the flutter of wings sounded quite close to the inlet.

There was a second's warning, a pinging sound, slight but adequate to warn the tense Marines.

"Grenade!" Lummis yelled.

The Marines ducked. The grenade exploded in the middle of the inlet.

"Incoming!" yelled Brannon. "Outgoing!" yelled the other Marine, as he jerked the loose pin out and lobbed the grenade out and over the bushes around him, like taking a hook shot with a basketball. The grenade landed with a soft splat in the swamp and there was a delay of a few seconds. The thrower was in the process of pitching another before the first grenade exploded. The other Marines had reacted. Fire poured into the swamp to the left.

Red lines of tracers cut back and forth from the dike to the water line. On the right flank, Brannon opened up with an automatic rifle after his buddy had thrown the grenades into the bush. The noise was deafening.

After about 10 seconds, they stopped firing. Someone cursed. The clatter of empty magazines being changed drowned out his voice. Lummis said in a low voice, "Knock it off and sit still. Listen for them. We probably got that one, so listen for groans or dragging sounds." "Anybody hit?"

"Yeh, Culver took some shrapnel. No big thing, though."

The Marines stopped what they were doing and waited. A flare opened over the river.

The grenade had been a ruse. The VC did not intend to stand and fight. While the firing was going on, some had tried to slip a boat past the inlet. The sudden silence had forced them to stop paddling. Before they could drift by, the mortar crew had fired illumination. They had to beach the boat on the sandbar.

The Marines loosed short bursts of concentrated fire. They could not see the Viet Cong, who might either have been lying in the shadows on the sandbar or swimming away. The Marines covered both areas. The arcs of the tracers enabled them to fire interlocking patterns almost as well as they could in daylight.

"Hey," Brannon shouted, "let me try for that boat with a LAAW. I never get a change to fire one." "All right, Brannon," Lummis answered, "but don't screw up. It's our only LAAW."

"Relax, I'm a pro," Brannon said. "Watch this."

Brannon extended the LAAW and knelt in the inlet near the spot where the incoming grenade had gone off. Sighting in carefully at the round wicker boat not 30 meters away, he squeezed the firing mechanism. Nothing happened. He realigned and squeezed again. Nothing. He tilted the tube upwards off his shoulder to inspect the faulty trigger. The LAAW went off with a roar, the rocket streaking out across the paddies like a howitzer shell.

"Great shooting," Lummis growled. "That'll land in district headquarters."

The patrol leader walked to the water's edge with his grenade launcher. He fired once and the M79 shell splintered the boat. "Let's go home," he said, "before we shoot down a jet."

<u>16 July 1966</u>. First Lieutenant Thomas J. O'Rourke, the executive officer of Charlie Company, had come to the fort. He was to advise for a few weeks and help where he could. The men looked forward to working with him. This was his second tour in Vietnam and his knowledge of tactics was deep. A well-known athlete, he had a reputation for aggressive action and a knack for massing his weapons in a fire fight.

Sullivan decided to go back to "The Head." There were not many good ambush spots and he wanted to show O'Rourke some action. Five Marines and two PFs comprised the patrol. As usual, a PF was placed at point. They left the fort at 2000.

When he entered the blackness of the main village street, the PF at point quickened the pace. O'Rourke, second in column, held to a slow, cautious tread. Seeing that he was all alone, the PF scurried back to the column and frantically gestured to the Marines to walk faster. The Marines ignored him. He returned to the point and went on more slowly.

From inside a house, the loud sound of forced coughing reached the Marines. The patrol stopped. The coughing stopped. The patrol proceeded. The coughing started again. The Marines were waiting for such a tip-off. They checked with the PF at point.

"Yes, yes, very bad man, number 10*. No VC himself but him warn VC," the PF said.

The PFs refused to apprehend the man. It was their village and their politics. They wanted the Marines to take some action. The Marines were willing.

---

*number 10 - Marine slang for a bad man or situation; its opposite is "number 1"

Three of them converged on the house. Lance Corporal Bettie walked to the open door. The Vietnamese inside looked at him for a moment and made a threatening gesture of hostility and contempt. Bettie didn't wait for the next move. He struck once and the man fell, spitting blood. Bettie leaned over him.

"When Marines pass, you no talk, you no cough." Bettie made a loud, false coughing sound. "You no warn V. C. no more. I come back sometime. I see."

The man nodded after every word. He understood. Perhaps the next time he would not cough; perhaps he would use a lantern. Or perhaps he would not. If he did, the Marines had orders to shoot out all blinking lights.

The Marines arrived at "The Head" and set in along the river bank. The rice paddies were to their backs and they were facing the river. They knew the VC had been alerted but their position could be easily defended.

By 2200, the traffic across the river was heavy. The Marines heard Vietnamese voices and splashes in the water. The night was overcast, however, and they could spot no movement.

It was instinct as much as sound that alerted O'Rourke. Someone was stalking them from the rear. He saw dark shadows. He watched. They did not move. Slowly he pulled his body over the bank, twisted around, and raised upon his elbows. Now he was facing to the rear with his back to the river. He checked the shadows again. They were closer to the Marines, not over 60 yards away. (Later, Lance Corporal Guadalupe Garcia told of glimpsing the infiltrators as they crept by his flank position. But he wasn't absolutely sure of what he saw and so he didn't report it to anyone.)

O'Rourke nudged Sullivan and Riley. They turned and looked. Riley, who could detect movement where most people would see nothing, whispered:

"Yes. Two of them."

The Marines wanted to wait until the VC had crept closer. They were given no waiting period, however. The two VC lost their nerve. Suddenly, they jumped up and ran diagonally away from the Marines. A Marine heaved a grenade at them. It travelled over 60 yards and exploded behind the VC.

O'Rourke, Sullivan, and Riley fired their automatic weapons in a long burst.

"I think I hit one," Riley said.

O'Rourke and Sullivan went forward to check. Sullivan went first, bending low and running hard until he reached a paddy dike. O'Rourke came up on his right, weaving as he ran. They found nobody. It was too dark to look for blood trails or gear which may have been dropped.

"This ambush is blown," said O'Rourke. "The VC are getting wise to us. We're just going to have to think these things through more. It's going to take more planning. Let's head back in."

<u>18 July 1966</u>. In an effort to break established patterns and keep the enemy off balance, Lieutenant O'Rourke altered the types and times of the patrols. On this night, four had gone out at dusk to set up ambushes. Two were sprung and all four patrols had returned to the fort before midnight. O'Rourke debriefed them and it appeared that another night's work had ended.

But at 0200, O'Rourke assembled eight Marines and left the fort. Riley took the point and the patrol headed for the village. They did not, however, use the main street or the side trails. Instead, they wandered through the backyards and hedgerows, moving parallel to the paths at a very slow pace. Riley picked the way with care, pausing every few steps to look and listen. O'Rourke had the patrol spread with the widest interval possible, just close enough so each man could distinguish the outline of the man in front of him. The patrol was in no hurry; they weren't going anywhere in particular. They would just rove through the village for a few hours, hunting for any VC who might have slipped in after the ambush patrols had returned to the fort.

After the Marines had roamed about for an hour without incident, O'Rourke decided to strike out southeast through some backyards to cross the main north-south trail where it was bisected by a path running due east. Thus, Riley chose a route which had the same general direction as the east path.

Cutting through backyards, Riley had almost reached the path when he halted. The patrol jerked up short and for several minutes nobody moved. Riley walked silently back to O'Rourke and whispered: "I thought I heard something on the path to our right. Did you?"

"I'm not sure," O'Rourke replied. "We were still moving when you stopped. Go ahead but take it slow."

They had proceeded at a creep for a few minutes when Riley halted, went down on his knees, placed his rifle on the ground, and flattened out. His head pointed toward the path six meters away. The other members of the patrol quietly lay down about 10 meters apart and faced in the same direction,

O'Rourke crawled to Riley's side.

"I know for sure I hear someone behind us. They're coming up this path." Riley whispered.

"Do you think they've heard us?" O'Rourke asked.

"No--too far away."

O'Rourke scooted back and warned the others. Sullivan and two other Marines pivoted about to protect the rear and right flank of the patrol. Riley, O'Rourke, and three other Marines faced the path and waited, having slipped off their safeties.

They heard the enemy approaching, not the steady noises of careless footsteps but the intermittent crunches and snaps of people walking cautiously but not cautiously enough. The middle of the path was obscured in dark shadows. The ambushers could not see any figures approaching; they could only gauge the distance by ear. O'Rourke thought he saw a man pass by him but he couldn't be sure. He heard another man getting close.

Not one of the Marines could remember who sprang the ambush. All were agreed that the four automatic rifles opened up within the same second. Swinging his weapon back and forth each Marine fired until he had emptied a magazine. It was strictly area fire at sounds. Not one Marine could actually see a target or be sure that he had hit anything. Then O'Rourke and Riley rose to their knees and heaved two grenades back down the trail in the direction from which the VCs had come.

"Cease fire!" O'Rourke yelled. "Riley, block for us to the front. A couple of you guys search the area."

The action had lasted eight seconds.

Corporal Lummis and Lance Corporal Larry Wingrove stepped out of the bushes, peering at the ground in front of them. Each found and searched a dead VC.

"Mine's clear," Lummis said.

"Mine too," said Wingrove.

"All right," O'Rourke said, "let's go home and get some rest. We'll go out again tomorrow night."

THE INDIANS

> Preface: At the end of July, the author spent a week with the 1st Force Reconnaissance Company, then operating from a task force headquarters at Dong Ha, 13 miles south of the Demilitarized Zone (DMZ) and 8 miles west of the South China Sea. He was the unnamed fifth member in the four-day reconnaissance patrol described in the story.

Sergeant Orest Bishko planned the patrol carefully. Along with other Force Reconnaissance units, his four-man team would go out on another scouting mission. For over a month they had been shadowing the 324B North Vietnamese Division. During the past two weeks, Marine rifle battalions, engaged in Operation HASTINGS, with heavy air and artillery support, had killed over 800 of the North Vietnamese. But many of the enemy were slipping away and retreating into the jungles. Reconnaissance Marines, like Sergeant Bishko, set out to find them.

Nothing about the mission was new to the men in his team. They had been on dozens of patrols in the hilly country north of Hue near the Demilitarized Zone. Major Dwain A. Colby, the company commander, had formulated four basic rules to be followed at all times. They were: (1) stay together no matter what happens; (2) upon reaching an observation post, call artillery fire upon a set of known coordinates so later fire missions can be called by shifting from a reference point; (3) maintain constant radio communications with headquarters; and (4) never stay in one spot more than 12 hours. The Marines could recite those rules in their sleep. Still Sergeant Bishko planned carefully. For, although he had been out on dozens of patrols, this was to be the first one he would lead.

The night before his team was to be set in, he briefed them, using a map and a written patrol order, stressing the importance of acting as a team out in the brush. He inspected the uniform and equipment of each man. They were ready.

The next morning, 26 July 1966, the men arose at 0400, applied black and green camouflage paint to their faces and arms, put on their packs and climbed on board a truck. They were driven to a nearby heli pad. Bishko talked to a pilot and showed him on a map exactly where the team should be dropped. The Marines climbed on board a Huey. Bishko put on a set of earphones.

Minutes later, the helicopter was skimming low down a long valley. It flew for several miles in a westerly direction, then Bishko said something into his mike and pointed to his right. The Huey banked sharply and dropped to the ground. The recon team leaped out and ran into the undergrowth. The Huey flew off down the valley, dipping down and hovering a few times in dummy landings to confuse any enemy who might have been watching. The Huey, called a "slick" because it carried passengers, not armament, was to stay on station a few ridgelines to the south for 30 minutes in case the team ran into trouble and needed to be extracted. Another Huey--this one a gunship, loaded with rockets and machine guns--was on call to provide fire support for such a pickup.

On the ground, Corporal William McWilliams, the team scout, assumed the point position. He was followed by Lance Corporal Thomas Moran, the radio operator, Bishko, another radioman, and the tail-end Charlie, Corporal Joel Miller.

The patrol headed for the high ground. The men jogged north out of the valley and started up the steep face of a ridgeline which ran in an east-west direction. They avoided the trails and stream beds, climbing steadily for several hours. Trees, bushes, thorns, and vines clogged the hill and their loads were heavy. Between them they carried two radios, 20 grenades, 1,200 rounds of ammunition, 20 canteens, and rations to last for 72 hours. Progress was slow.

But the weather favored them. It was overcast and cool, with a high wind blowing and thick clouds hiding the hot sun which sapped a man's strength so quickly.

By noon they reached a clump of trees on a nose of the hill and from there they could see the valley floor. They settled down to wait and watch. One man scanned the valley with binoculars while another listened to the rear. Visibility into the brush was less than 15 feet but a man listening intently could hear noises made 1,000 meters away. The other Marines dozed. They alternated sentinel duty every hour or two.

McWilliams heard the enemy first. He whispered a warning to the others. "Listen up. They're in there behind us." They strained to hear. They filtered out the ordinary sounds, the far away jet or artillery, the low buzz of crickets, the stirring of branches when the wind passed. They listened for the unusual.

They heard it, an intermittent pounding noise made by something heavy striking into the earth, coming from above them, farther along the ridgeline back towards the mountain.

"What is it?"

"I don't know, but it sure isn't any elephant, so you guess who's sounding off."

A while later, they heard someone chopping wood in the same general area.

As dusk approached, the team prepared to move, having seen no one and heard no more sounds. Behind the knob where the Marines sat, the top of the ridgeline slanted north and sliced back south to form an inverted V, before turning eastward again. Rather than follow along the top in what would be the normal route of traffic, Bishko decided to cut cross-compartment and move west, down one side of the cut, across a stream bed, and up 600 feet to the other side, a route so steep and thick that he thought the chances were remote they would be seen or heard.

The hike took over two hours and when the Marines reached level ground again on the ridgeline they were exhausted and their clothes soaked with sweat. They squeezed, pushed, and jerked their way into the thickest brush they could find and established a harbor site for the night.

Each man scraped the ground bare where he would lie down, so that if he heard something during the night, he could alert the others and set up a defense without giving away his position. The Marines ate from cold cans of rations and spoke only when necessary, and then in brief whispers. They arranged alternate two hour watches. The light faded quickly.

With the dark, the enemy began moving. Vietnamese voices floated up to the Marines from the stream bed they had just crossed. Bishko called a fire mission, requesting a three round salvo. From the sound of the explosion a few minutes later, the Marines judged the 105mm shells had hit close to the voices. That night the men slept fitfully, uneasy about the high wind which could cover the movement of an enemy.

At dawn, Bishko pointed out a section of high ground to the west where he wished to set up an observation post. The map distance measured 700 meters and the ridgeline ran straight to it.

It took the Marines four hours to reach their destination. They avoided the bare, conspicuous ridge crest and traversed the rain-slicked shoulder of the hill. From past patrols they had grown calluses on the sides of their feet, so often had they half walked, half slipped their way along mountain sides. Although thirsty, they conserved their water, knowing that the five canteens per man had to last four days.

When the team finally clawed up to the selected spot, a knoll covered with chest-high elephant grass, McWilliams and Miller crawled forward to observe; Bishko and Moran waited on the reverse slope. Jutting out at a point where the ridgeline hooked abruptly from a westerly to a northerly direction, the knoll provided an excellent field of observation for several miles up the valley to the west. The valley, a half-mile wide at that point, held fields of dry, tall grass and scrub brush and arbors of dense trees; it funneled 20 miles back into Laos and served as a main avenue of approach for the enemy into Quang Tri Province.

The Marines saw their first VC during midafternoon. Two North Viets in khaki uniforms crossed a stream down in the valley a quarter of a mile from the Marines. They walked across a bamboo bridge laughing and joking as if they were in their own backyard. McWilliams and Miller were startled by their closeness. They had scoured the distant trails for over an hour and were not entirely pleased to find the enemy under their noses. Their vantage point gave little concealment, only a few scraggly bushes and the rippling grass. They froze for several minutes in rigid concentration before deciding that the angle of vision and the careless manner of the North Vietnamese made their discovery unlikely. McWilliams then slipped back over the slope to the niche where Bishko sat watching to the rear.

"Sergeant," he whispered, "company to the front--two of them."

Bishko and Moran crept forward, relieved McWilliams and Miller of the watch, and spent some time just familiarizing themselves with the valley floor in relation to the map. Bishko pinpointed the coordinates of the bamboo bridge and settled down to wait, paying close attention to the bridge, which was not more than 20 feet long. Tall trees and tangles of vines overhung the southern bank of the stream, while the northern bank looked like it had been cut away by flash floods and was now a gravel wash, which sloped upwards for 10 meters before merging into a grove of dense trees. The knob where the team perched was 150 feet above the stream.

Just before dusk, six more North Vietnamese ambled over the bridge and entered the grove. Three were dressed in Khaki and three wore black pajamas; none carried arms.

"Looks like a force of North Vietnamese with local guides," Bishko whispered. "Moran, get out a fire mission."

The artillery strike was off. Despite a few adjustments, the rounds did not hit near the target. The artillery battery, dug in five miles due east, had to raise the muzzles of their howitzers at a high angle in order to fire the 105mm shells up over the ridgeline and down into the valley. But a strong wind was blowing the shells off course as they wavered at their apexes before plunging down.

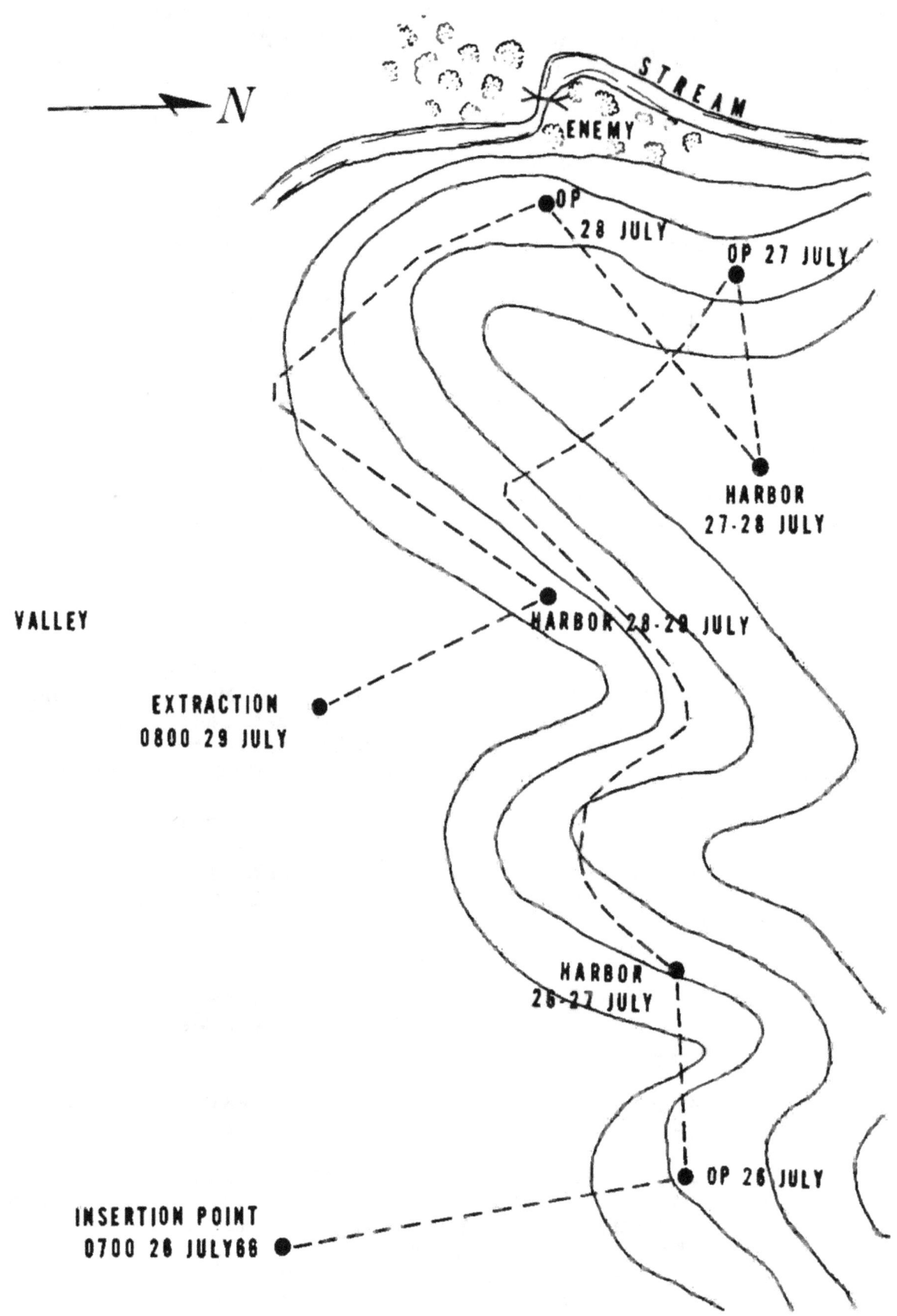

SCHEMATIC SKETCH TO ACCOMPANY "THE INDIANS"

"Tell them to cease fire. We'll try again in the morning when the wind has died."

For a harbor site that night, Bishko chose a thicket of grass and dry bamboo, so strewn with dry leaves that a crawling snake could be heard. Miller concealed their back trail. They cleared away some leaves and lay down just at dark. It rained on and off during the night, but the Marines not on watch didn't notice; they would have slept treading water.

At first light, when the sky to the east was glowing red, the team left the harbor site. They travelled straight down the hill through the grass, knowing they could not be seen in the dim light. Bishko led them to a small clump of trees which was slightly nearer to the bamboo bridge than their vantage point the day before.

At dawn the enemy began stirring. The sounds of their conversations carried plainly to the Marines, but none crossed the bridge and the Marines could not see through the green canopy of trees. The grove extended 300 meters north and was about 100 meters wide, bordered on the east by the ridgeline where the patrol was hiding. The stream ran from the north along the west side of the grove, then jinked sharply east toward the ridgeline. Over the stream where it bent east the enemy had built their bridge. Bishko believed there were probably a dozen North Vietnamese encamped in the grove below him and decided to call for artillery again.

"Hateful, this is Primness," Moran whispered into the PRC 25 radio. "Fire Mission. Concentration Papa India five zero niner. Voices in stream bed. One round. Willy Peter. Will adjust."

From his position, Bishko could clearly see the bridge and stream. The stream curled gradually to the right and heavy foliage covered both banks. The voices were coming from the right bank in a clump of tall trees.

"On the way," whispered Moran. The artillery round hurtled in over the Marines' heads. It sounded like someone ripping cloth. The explosion was sharp and close. A cloud of white smoke drifted up. From the grove of trees two VC emerged clad in khaki shorts and khaki shirts and casually walked south across the bridge.

"Have them come left one hundred and fire for effect," whispered Bishko.

A few minutes later the rounds came tearing in. The grove shook with the successive explosions. Fifteen North Vietnamese came out from the trees and walked rapidly to the stream crossing, and waded across.

"Hit them with a couple of more volleys," Bishko whispered.

Twelve more rounds smashed into the trees, the sound of the explosions mingling into one continuous roar.

About 40 enemy ran from the grove. They scampered to the stream and splashed across as fast as they could, dressed in a variety of ways: some in khaki, some in khaki shirts and black shorts, some in gray shirts and blue shorts, some in black pajamas, some even in light blue pajamas.

"Keep that fire coming. Call for area fire and hit the other bank," Bishko whispered. The reconnaissance team had discovered the base camp of a mixed VC/North Vietnamese battalion.

McWilliams tried to count the enemy as they forded the stream. He tallied 75; then they were pouring across the stream faster than he could count. Bishko could not tabulate an accurate figure either.

"Tell them there are more than 200 that we can see at one point. Have them pour it on."

The shells slammed down in random patterns on both sides of the streams, felling trees and more North Vietnamese. A group of the enemy waded back across the stream, holding bamboo poles. Other soldiers followed them, holding high above the water bunches of white bandages. They ran across the gravel wash back into the grove and some minutes later trotted back carrying their wounded and dead slung beneath the poles. Others scurried about, hauling packs bulging with supplies. Some ran upstream clutching armfuls of weapons.

The artillery pounded them relentlessly. The enemy seemed to lose their sense of purpose and direction. Some staggered like punchdrunk fighters. Others threw down their packs and ran. There was mass panic and confusion in the stream bed.

A few dozen heavily armed men splashed through the stream bed and disappeared from view on the Marines' right flank. The team could hear them crashing through the brush, coming up the slope. Some Vietnamese leader had determined that the bombardment was too continuous and accurate to be merely a lucky burst of harassing fire. At least one group of the enemy were organized and purposeful. They were searching for the team.

Another volley dropped into the grove. Still more of the enemy rushed out. Some were bent over, carrying wounded on their backs. Staying together in one large group, they started to wade the stream.

Another volley. Three of the shells exploded in the stream. The enemy disappeared from the Marines' view in a shower of spray, mud, and stones. When the debris had settled, McWilliams could see no North Vietnamese who were still moving. Some were floating face down in the stream, others were lying in twisted shapes along the bank, a few were hanging from vines several yards in the air. The bamboo bridge sagged to water level under the weight of several collapsed enemy. Bodies clogged the stream and turned its color to rust.

The team could not stay to call in any more fire. The search party was not 30 meters downslope. Bishko scrambled up the hill and gathered his men.

"Let's move out. They're coming up the hill after us." He paused to catch his breath.

"But I'll tell you, we've just killed a hell of a lot of them."

They went down the back of the hill through the grass in loping strides, passing where a 105mm shell had fallen short and clipped yards of grass off at the roots as evenly as a scythe. McWilliams found a stream bed and led the team down into its protecting shadows.

They arrived out of breath and uncertain of their future at the bottom of the hill on the opposite side from the North Vietnamese camp. They collapsed where they stood and struggled to regain their wind, feeling they could rely only on their physical condition and knowledge of woodcraft to elude those who chased them. Back at task force headquarters, the S-3 of the reconnaissance company, Captain William S. Ostrie, had listened to their whispers over the radio and heard the situation develop. He acted to provide them immediate and powerful support. The pilot of an Air Force observation plane was contacted and asked to fly up the valley toward the Marines' position and to provide what assistance he could. That pilot, in turn, guided in a Marine jet, which had been diverted from its primary target by Ostrie's call for emergency aid for the reconnaissance patrol.

The patrol members themselves were completely unaware of this rapid, saving chain of events. But, while still breathing hard and lying at the base of the hill, they did hear the soft single-engine putter of the tiny Air Force plane and seconds later saw it flying directly toward them, not 50 feet above the ground. Bishko stood up and waved and flashed a signal mirror at the plane. The pilot wagged his wings in recognition and spoke to Moran over the patrol's radio frequency. In broken sentences, Moran explained their plight. "They're right behind us," he said. "On the hill, and their base camp's on the other side, where the bodies are."

"Roger," said the pilot. "I'll take a look."

He circled once over the stream bed and reported he counted 50 bodies. (McWilliams though there were 53.) Buzzing the hill, he caught a glimpse of the North Vietnamese. That was all he needed. He radioed to Moran, warning the Marines to seek cover. The enemy was closing rapidly behind them and he did not have time to waste.

The members of the patrol never saw the jet. One minute they were listening intently for sounds of their pursuers and the next minute the air was filled with a sharp screeching. It was the sound of an F-8 Crusader hurtling down at 300 mph with a 2,000-pound bomb slung under each wing. Captain Orson G. Swindle, III, sat at the controls concentrating intently on the observation pilot's instructions.

"Hit 50 meters at 12 o'clock on my smoke on a holding of 270°."

Swindle could see the hill, the stream bed, the gravel wash, and the thin white smoke wisps of the observations pilot's marking rockets. The target was plain, but Swindle was uneasy, for the Air Force pilot had warned him the reconnaissance patrol was only 400 meters from the smoke markers. Swindle had dropped 1,000-pound bombs 700 meters in front of friendly lines and considered that close enough. Swindle held his craft very steady and released the two bombs simultaneously. He came out of his 30° dive at 1,800 feet, pulling 5 G's very smartly. The bombs fell free and plummeted down, thick, stubby, menacing hulks painted a dull green and repulsive even to look at.

They struck and the blast jolted the Marines crouched on the other side of the hill. The ground jumped under their feet. For seconds they could hear nothing, while a high ringing sound filled their ears. They looked at each other, gaping, not quite sure what had happened. Dirt, boulders, and the limbs of trees began falling around them. They dove for cover under the trees and hoped the debris would miss them.

Miller whispered: "That stuff could kill you just as quick as a bullet."

Moran got on the radio and whispered furiously. "You missed. You almost hit us. Hit the other side. Hit the top. But don't hit here!"

A calm voice replied. "Relax. He was right on target. Nobody's behind you now. But you have to expect some fallout when you're that close to those blockbusters."

The observation pilot was right. The pursuers were no more. The patrol turned east and toiled slowly around the shoulder of the ridge and harbored in a deep draw, hoping to find another suitable observation post. In this endeavor they did not succeed. But fatigue did not overcome caution. McWilliams and Miller took turns climbing a tall tree to watch their back trail. Late in the afternoon, their vigilance was rewarded. The enemy came, casting for tracks and shouting loudly back and forth.

Moran called for artillery. Volley after volley smashed in, and the valley echoed and reechoed the rolling thunder for many minutes. Bishko listened to the din and smiled. "That artillery," he whispered, "is just like having a guardian angel." The Marines neither saw nor heard any more North Vietnamese that afternoon.

They had difficulty keeping awake on watch that night. They dared not stamp their feet or move around; they were on the verge of exhaustion. By dint of sheer determination, Bishko stayed alert throughout most of the night to ensure the others would not doze off.

The next morning, a helicopter swooped in to pick them up. With signal mirrors they guided the pilot into the landing zone, then clambered happily on board and flew to task force headquarters for debriefing. There they were told they had called in one of the most successful artillery missions on record thus far in the Vietnamese war. The Marines were so tired they could hardly smile. Corporal McWilliams chose that moment to look at his old friend and say: "That's not half bad, Sergeant--for your first time, that is."

Then they smiled, close comrades sharing an in-joke.

TALKING FISH

Preface: After leaving the 1st Force Reconnaissance Company, the author visited India Battery of the 12th Marines at the end of July to determine their reaction to the exceptional fire support they provided Bishko's patrol. After several hours with those men, observing, questioning, and taping, it became obvious to him that he would be doing artillery an injustice if he merely mentioned them in a few sentences as an adjunct to another story. Here is what the Marines of India Battery did in the 24-hour period which included their support of the reconnaissance patrol.

I

For the men of India Battery, the shooting day generally reached its heaviest peak at night. During the hours of darkness, the howitzers would unleash harassment and interdiction fires at dozens of points. These rounds fell unobserved by the Marines, exploding in random patterns throughout enemy territory. The purpose of such missions was to disrupt the movements of the North Vietnamese, to cause them anxiety and lack of rest, and to deny them the secure use of trails and stream beds.

In mid-July, India Battery, with six howitzers and 73 men, had been transported by helicopters to a valley some four miles southwest of Dong Ha, near the Demilitarized Zone. From this valley, the battery fired in support of units from the 4th Marines, 5th Marines, and the 1st Force Reconnaissance Company, all engaged in Operation HASTINGS.

On 27 July, Battery I had barely begun to fire its H&I missions when the routine was interrupted by a radio request for a fire mission. The message was sent from "Kalamazoo 66," a forward observer team attached to the 3d Battalion, 5th Marines. The target designated was "moving lights on hillside."

At 2016, the howitzers opened fire on the target. After two adjustments, a fire-for-effect was called in and the six howitzers fired five high-explosive rounds apiece, each shell weighing 33 pounds. Secondary explosions followed the impact, indicating that the 105mm shells had triggered the detonation of enemy ammunition or fuel.

The lights hovered and wavered in the blackness, then slowly bobbed back up the mountain. A shift from the last fire-for-effect was called and again the shells rustled down on the lights. There were more secondary explosions and the lights went out. The men at the battery waited. After a delay of several minutes, the lights reappeared farther up the mountain. Another shift. More salvos. More secondary explosions. And still once more after that, the process was repeated before the lights winked on the skyline and disappeared. The battery had fired for 29 minutes on the mission and expended 134 shells.

During those fire missions, another forward observer team (Kalamazoo 61) had monitored the radio and followed on a map the slow retreat of the enemy. Their position was on the valley floor on the other side of the mountain from Kalamazoo 66. By simple deduction and proper use of a map and compass, they were able to focus their attention on a spot in the blackness where they suspected the enemy were. Fifteen minutes passed and they saw nothing. But at 2100 a speck of light glowed through the foliage. Having pinpointed the coordinates, they called for an immediate fire-for-effect and the battery responded with 12 high-explosive rounds. When the forward observer team counted more than 12 explosions, they notified the battery of that fact, and requested a repeat of the mission. Again the battery fired a dozen rounds, this time mixing in white phosporous shells. A few more secondary explosions followed and the team could see the lights no longer.

The battery returned to the conduct of ordinary H&I fires. The forward observer team remained on watch. Forty minutes elapsed--then lights again glimmered on the shoulders of the mountain. The team quickly notified the battery, which suspended the H&I missions and threw 18 high-explosive shells on the lights. The shells struck, setting off a secondary explosion so powerful it lit up the entire mountainside. At the gun pits, 4,200 meters away, the battery commander, Captain Burr Chambless, looked at the bright flash on the horizon and shouted to his section chiefs: "You goofed up. What are you firing Willie Peter for?"

The NCOs assured him they had not and the Marines of the battery began to discuss eagerly the nature and size of the target they had destroyed. But no immediate survey of the damage by infantrymen was possible. At night in the jungle, close surveillance of artillery strikes is foregone.

The next day, on both sides of the mountain, patrols discovered bloody shreds of clothing and helmets. They reported that patches of the jungle which had been ripped by the artillery smelled of death. The twisted casings of a few enemy 120mm mortar shells and bits of an iron wheel were found.

The North Vietnamese probably had intended to drag the heavy weapons into a safe defilade position away from the ridgeline, which was vulnerable to air and artillery strikes. They most likely had calculated that the dense canopy would shield their lights from the sight of the Marines. They were wrong.

The first forward observer team (Kalamazoo 66) to see the lights was able to adjust fire on the target. At night, when distances are hard to estimate accurately and the jungle smothers the sound and dims the flash from adjusting rounds, this was no mean feat. The other forward observer team (Kalamazoo 61) showed good sense in tracking the fire mission and skill in adjusting its initial fire missions on target so swiftly. Both teams remained alert even after the lights went out. Had either team assumed the shoot was over after their initial fires-for-effect met with success, the damage to the enemy would have been much less severe. Both had obviously pinpointed their respective map positions and acquainted themselves with the surrounding terrain while it was still light.

II

Having averaged four to six hours of punctuated sleep, the men were back at the guns in the morning when a radio message came in under the call sign "Hateful." Hateful was the code word for a radio station operated by the 1st Force Reconnaissance Company. The station was perched on a peak high above the valley floor and relayed messages from long-range reconnaissance patrols back to the task force headquarters and artillery batteries.

The relay station passed on to India Battery a fire mission from "Primness." Chambless recognized the call sign. It was a small reconnaissance patrol located deep in the jungle for whom the battery had fired several missions during the past two days.

The target was designated as "voices in stream bed." Chambless was puzzled by the vague term but he did not question it. That wasn't his job. He had confidence in the judgment of the Marines on patrol. The reconnaissance Marines had been trained in forward observer procedures by the S-3 of the battalion --Major Barry Bittner. They did not call fire foolishly.

But an officer on the staff of one of the rifle battalions Chambless was also supporting did think the mission foolish. Having monitored the radio message from Hateful, he called Chambless, sarcastically asking if the battery had the time and ammunition to waste on voices and bushes. Chambless replied that his battery directly supported the reconnaissance patrol and that, yes, he was going to fire the mission.

But the artillery Fire Direction Center (FDC) was momentarily stumped. The patrol's compass azimuth to the target had been sent in code so a listening enemy could not locate their position. This shackle system garbled the numbers of the azimuth and the battery did not have the key to that particular code. Staff Sergeant John E. Williams, the operations chief, solved the problem by radioing a nearby rifle battalion, which unscrambled the numbers.

Four minutes had been wasted. The computers--men trained to compute the technical data necessary to aim the guns--went to work. Lance Corporal F. C. Puskoskie called out his fire data computations first. Lance Corporal William J. Garrison studied his figures and yelled "check." Five minutes had gone by.

Next, Sergeant John Dovale called the artillery liaison officer on duty at the operations tent of the task force. The artillery liaison officer jotted down the coordinates of the Marines' and the enemy's positions, the azimuth of fire, and the height the 105 shells would travel in the air. He took this information to the air liaison officer standing watch in the same tent and requested a "Save-A-Plane" number. Until aircraft were warned to stay clear of the area through which the artillery shells would pass in flight, the mission could not be fired.

The battery did not just sit idle and wait. The firing data was transmitted over the telephone wire to the executive pit.

"Battery -- adjust.

Action Rear.

Shell Willie Peter.

Charge 6.

Fuze Quick.

Center -- one round.

Battery -- one round.

Shell H.E.

High angle.

In effect.

Deflection 2457.

Quadrant 1130."

On the map, no more than 300 meters separated the reconnaissance patrol from the target. The patrol was crouched on a hill 200 feet above the stream bed. To hit the target and miss the Marines, the Fire Direction Officer, Second Lieutenant Dixon Kelley, plotted a high-angle shoot. When adjusted to fire the mission, the howitzer tubes pointed almost straight up in the air. This would throw the shells high so that, having peaked, they would plummet almost straight down. Thus, the artillery rounds would miss the hill but hit the target.

The previous afternoon the Primness patrol had requested the same fire mission. A high wind, blowing in erratic gusts, had played havoc with the prolonged flight of the shells. The patrol was forced to hastily cancel the mission when the adjustments fell wide of their intended marks.

There was no wind early on the morning of 28 July. Still Kelley was wary. He did not relish putting precise measurements at the whim of a puff of air.

The battery executive officer, First Lieutenant Charles W. Cheatham, told his phone man to pass on to the guns the data he had received from the FDC. This added step was a safety procedure, because it insured a doublecheck to verify the data placed on the guns. Cheatham added a twist to the routine.

"Tell the guns the target is talking fish," he said.

The artillerymen appreciated the humor. It was a good ploy which revived the spirits of tired men. They laughed and joked as they readied the guns. Perhaps recon had been left out in the jungles too long this time.

Private First Class Raymond O. Tindell carried a white phosporous shell from the ammunition pit to gun #4. Private First Class N. C. Sheble loaded the round into the breech, while Private First Class David L. Sherburne aligned the gun according to the fire data. Lance Corporal Henry H. Smalley grasped the rope lanyard and waited. He would fire the first adjusting round of the mission. He was bored. He thought it was the beginning of another futile effort. The VCs would slip away and the patrol would report back to the battery that there had been one or two enemy wounded.

The section chief, Sergeant Bobby M. Goodnight, checked the lay of the gun and shouted: "Gun 4 up."

Seven minutes had elapsed since the fire mission request came in. A call came into the Fire Direction Center from the artillery liaison officer at task force: "Save-a-plane number 28-Bravo."

The planes had been alerted to the fire mission. If a pilot had to cross through the area, he would fly his plane (or helicopter) at a higher altitude than the peak of the arc of the artillery shells.

"Fire."

Eight minutes after receiving the fire mission, the first artillery round was on its way to target. Another 48 seconds would pass before the round landed. Captain Chambless was dissatisfied with that amount of time. Staff Sergeant Williams was dissatisfied. The crew of gun 4 was dissatisfied.

"Too damn long," Chambless growled. The communications snag and the delay in clearance irritated the whole battery. They prided themselves on fast, accurate shooting. Chambless made a notation to mention the mixup in shackle sheets at the next pre-patrol meeting. (Before an insertion, the reconnaissance team leader visited with his artillery support officer. Together they preplanned fires and set procedures and also discussed past mistakes made.)

Primness called in a correction.

"Left one hundred--fire one volley for effect." The first round had exploded near the target. The computers were waiting. They worked quickly and fed the data corrections to the guns.

Less than two minutes later the six-round volley was on its way. The battery waited--set to compute and adjust for another correction.

No correction came. Instead the FOC heard: "Repeat fire for effect. Eight VCs seen crossing stream."

Another volley was fired. The men in the battery were no longer bored. Having learned they were firing at observed targets, their interest naturally heightened. Hateful relayed another message from Primness.

"Left 200, add 100. A platoon of VCs seen running upstream. Request three volleys."

Again the artillerymen fired--and wondered. The talking fish seemed to be multiplying.

Another relay call from Primness reached the battery. "Request area saturation fire. Two hundred VCs moving across stream bed."

The gun crews fired, reloaded, realigned, and fired, again and again. Small shifts were phoned to the guns to insure the shells did not land on top of one another.

A final message came from Primness.

"Cease fire. FO cannot observe. He has been chased off the hill."

It was 0800. In 40 minutes, India Battery had fired 1,749 pounds of high explosives into an area 400 meters wide and 300 meters deep. They waited expectantly for a surveillance of the mission. None came. The men were disappointed. (Not until late in the afternoon did the battery learn 50 enemy bodies were counted lying in the stream bed after the artillery struck. What had happened under the canopy of trees could not be seen. Sergeant Goodnight said, "We felt really happy when we heard the results. It made you feel like you were over here doing something.")

The coordination, clearance, and communication problems pertaining to Marine artillery support in Vietnam were so formidable at that time that personal liaison between the supporting battery and the unit to be supported became advisable, and it was standing operating procedure for reconnaissance units to brief the artillery battery before a patrol went out. Even so, the fire mission had come perilously close to never being fired at all. The mixup in shackle sheets could have prevented decoding if Staff Sergeant Williams had not immediately contacted other units to obtain the information needed.

Chambless made every effort to keep his men informed as to the nature of the target and the patrol's situation. When a damage surveillance was not radioed back to the battery at the end of the mission, he checked with other sources to find out if the artillery proved helpful, and if so, what it did. He did not neglect the morale of his men.

III

When the Primness patrol could no longer call in fire, the men stood down from the guns but they did not rest; there was ammunition to haul and store. The helicopters whirled in to dump out hundreds of boxes of shells. The resupply kept the men busy hauling by hand (and one mechanical mule) 108,000 pounds of ammunition from the helicopter landing zone to the gun pits, some hundreds of meters away. It was an all-day job.

(But for sheer Hurculean effort, the labors of the Marines loading helicopters in the Logistic Support Area deserve special mention. There were 20 of them assigned to work the main supply point at Dong Ha for the duration of Operation HASTINGS. Grimy, black-faced, built like bulls, they worked steadily and impassively at their jobs for 15 days, trudging back and forth daily across the same patch of brown earth, loading by hand the helicopters, and chewing the dust the rotating blades swept up. A glance at the supply manifest and a few casual questions showed some startling statistics. They usually hauled cargos from 0500 one morning until 0100 the next morning, moving between 120,000 and 160,000 pounds of supplies a day.)

The battery fired a few more missions during the day, chiefly in support of the Primness patrol. The patrol had melted into the jungle after their engagement with the North Vietnamese battalion but stayed near the ravaged enemy base camp, hoping to direct another artillery or air strike. Instead, they were almost struck themselves. The North Vietnamese, after a lull of several hours while they reorganized, conducted a search for them.

Running off the hill, the Marines had left a trail through the dry grass that a native of New York City could follow. The patrol leader had anticipated the possibility of trackers. When the trackers came casting along the backtrail, they were heard and located by the patrol. The patrol leader radioed that information, together with the coordinates of the enemy, to the relay station. The station notified the battery.

This time the battery did not have to wait for a decoding key. Less than two minutes after reception of the message, the guns were firing. So swift was the reaction that the message alerting the patrol of an impending fire mission reached the patrol via the relay station after the shells had fallen. The battery fired 1,188 pounds of high explosives to discourage the trackers. It did.

Twenty minutes later, from task force headquarters came the order to blanket the entire target area. At higher headquarters, the thinking was that, if the North Vietnamese had organized a pursuit, they must have returned to their base camp and been in the process of digging out. The battery fired another area saturation mission, dropping 10,692 pounds of high explosives in the stream bed, base camp, and hill complex.

That night--28 July--the battery engaged the enemy at much closer range. Nestled in a small valley, the battery perimeter was linked with that of a rifle company. This relieved in large measure the problem of a local defense, since Captain Chambless was charged with protecting only a small sector of the perimeter around the guns.

It was that sector the enemy probed. Chambless had set out in the jungle three three-man listening posts. These posts were arranged in a triangular shape, placed deep enough in the underbrush to prevent the enemy from throwing grenades into the perimeter. At 2215, the Viet Cong attacked the outposts with grenades and small arms fire. Over a dozen grenades were thrown at the Marines, but all fell well short of the foxholes. The Marines in their turn threw grenades, fired their rifles semiautomatically, and fired the M79 grenade launcher. The entire action lasted less than 15 minutes. No Marine was wounded. No known damage was inflicted on the enemy. But it was not a random effort on the part of the VC. It was a deliberate probe to see if the artillerymen would react foolishly or timidly to close-in harassment. Having found this did not occur, the VC withdrew.

They came back two hours later. This time they climbed to the top of a small ridgeline some 300 meters from the gun positions. From there they opened fire with four automatic weapons, aiming at the flashes from the muzzles of the howitzers. Simultaneously, small parties of the enemy attempted to outflank the outposts. Two separate actions developed.

The nine Marines on outpost duty fought with grenades. Their triangular defense provided mutual support and, when the enemy tried to slip around the point outpost, they were pinned down by the outpost to the rear and had to pull back. Unable to budge the outposts and receiving two grenades for each one they threw, the enemy gave up the attempt and withdrew.

Those manning the automatic weapons on the ridgeline proved more stubborn. Captain Chambless had taken the precaution of zeroing in a .50 caliber machine gun on the ridgeline during the day. When the battery positions came under fire, he ordered one crew to return fire with that weapon. The VC were not impressed. Their fire poured in unabated.

The artillerymen, far from being intimidated, were enjoying the action. Although bullets were snapping by all gun positions, no Marine had been seriously wounded and the element of danger came as a welcome respite to the tedium of endless H&I fires. But Chambless was exasperated. To him, the grenade probes and machine gun fire were irritating impediments to the conduct of efficient battery fires. Determined to dislodge the enemy and discourage them as much as possible, he directed one gun crew to take the ridgeline under direct fire with the howitzer. Sighting in on the muzzle flashes of the enemy weapons, the crew fired six shells in quick succession at the VC position. That ended the fire fight and the battery began conducting H&I missions.

It was the start of another day's shoot.

AN HONEST EFFORT

> Preface: When the author visited 2/5 early in July, the battalion commander, Lieutenant Colonel Walter Moore, suggested that he spend some time with the men of Echo Company, who had been fighting hard in a wide valley for over a month. For several days, the author stayed with that company. When the fighting died down, a civic action program had been started, an effort in which the men took more interest and devoted more energy as it grew.

Captain Jim Cooper was tired. He was tired of climbing to the high ground, of sitting in the hot sun, of skirmishing inconclusively with guerrillas in the valley, and then returning to defend bare ridgelines.

His command, Echo Company of the 5th Marines, had established a combat outpost on Hill 76, the dominating terrain feature in the center of a large valley 10 miles west of Chulai. Each day the Marines sallied forth in platoon strength. The patrols passed through the hamlets and villages, clusters of wooden huts surrounded by trees and thickets. Between the hamlets stretched acres of rice paddies, stagnant fields without shade. The hills bordering the valley were covered by thick brush and dry grass which trapped the heat and stopped any breeze.

The day patrols rarely encountered any Viet Cong. The Marines would climb slowly back up Hill 76 at dusk to man the perimeter and sleep. The hill was bare of trees and the Marines joked that there was more dust than air.

Night ambushes went out, setting in along the main trails leading from the mountains into the hamlets. Contact was frequent but kills few. The Viet Cong moved in small groups and, when fired upon, dispersed instantly.

The enemy controlled the hamlets. This was obvious to the Marines. When a patrol passed, the children rarely waved and the villagers stayed within their houses. Scattered along the trails in front of them, Marines often found fresh leaflets showing pictures of wounded Americans and printed messages saying: "Protest the war before this happens to you." Occasionally, the enemy tried to ambush the Marines as they left the tree line bordering a hamlet. This tactic was not successful because each patrol left a machine gun team behind as security when the patrol had to cross the rice paddies. The local Vietnamese Popular Forces company never ventured outside their fort at night.

The presence of the Marines did deny to large main-force enemy units free access to the valley. It did not, however, prevent the Viet Cong infrastructure, the local and political forces of the enemy, from maintaining surveillance and control of the villagers.

After a few weeks of fruitless forays and grimy living, Echo Company changed its tactics and position. "I just got plain sick and tired of baking on top of some hill while the VC ran the villagers down in the valleys. So I decided to move," Captain Cooper said.

The company walked off the hill and into the hamlet of Thanh My Trung. Cooper arranged his defensive positions with care. They did not infringe on the villagers' houses or property but they were well within the hamlet itself. The Marines now had shade, water, and level sleeping ground.

The villagers were flabbergasted. Cooper called a meeting of the entire hamlet. Over 250 men, women, and children gathered to hear what he had to say. Cooper was big and blunt. It was his third war. He had started as a private. He had come to Vietnam to fight, not to pamper people.

He told the villagers so. He told them he had come to stay and they wouldn't have to fear the Viet Cong any longer. He told them to tell the VC he had come, so they would have time to run away, since they were afraid to fight. And he told them they were looking at the hardest man alive, if they helped the VC fight one of his Marines.

The company established a routine. Patrols became more frequent but of shorter length and duration. Each platoon was responsible for its own security. The number of night ambushes was increased and the number of contacts gradually diminished until, during the month of July, the company's tactical area of responsibility quieted completely and not even one large fire fight was recorded. Even snipers were very rare, and, although difficulties with mines persisted, no booby trap was ever found in Thanh My Trung.

The Marines, long covered with dust, splashed often in the ample water. They shaved daily and soaped down and rinsed off in the evenings. Soap was given to the villagers and they were urged to use it. At first, the villagers scrubbed their clothes but not themselves.

It was the children who led the way. Natural mimics and completely unafraid of the Marines, they swarmed each morning and evening, anxious to show the Marines they could bathe too.

The Villagers followed suit slowly. Hospitalman 3d Class Louis I. Piatetsky, the chief corpsman in the company, was insistent that any villager who asked for medical aid was told to wash before he would be treated. The Marines yelled loudly and forcefully every time they saw soap squandered on clothes.

Medical treatments also started with the children. They ran to the Marines for comfort and help with skinned knees, cut feet, and scraped elbows. Seeing the attention and care their children received, the villagers came forward. Their diseases and wounds were more serious. Medical evacuations for Vietnamese civilians from Thanh My Trung became a daily occurrence. The corpsmen were kept busy each day. Piatetsky's knowledge of the Vietnamese language lent order where otherwise chaos would have existed. The Vietnamese could explain what hurt them and be understood. Piatetsky himself, in one month (July), treated over 500 Vietnamese. Each week a doctor and a dentist visited the hamlet. During July they recorded 480 cases in their logs.

The hamlet of Thanh My Trung had a population of less than 360. The entire village numbered about 6,000. The Marines were amazed at how the news travelled from the valley, but they were sure many of those treated were not local villagers. The success of the program pleased the battalion's civil affairs officer, Captain Herbert R. Edson. "Look at it this way," he said, "the more concrete and immediate our help to the people is--things they can grasp and understand right here and now--the more we're undercutting the appeal and authority of the Viet Cong infrastructure in this same area."

The social life of Thanh My Trung revolved around the daily hot meal of the Marines. Somehow the Marines never ate quite all their food. There was always a little left for the children. Af first, chow call looked like a circus. The Marines would finish eating, then line up at the concertina wire to watch the fun. Amidst the cheers of the Marines, the cooks and the company gunnery sergeant would charge forth to set up a chow line. Gunnery Sergeant Jack R. Montera would bellow and rant and rave for order in his best Bronx manner. The children would giggle and swarm around him, intent only on the food. The cooks would try to dole out equal helpings to all. But so many small hands holding palm leaves would thrust forward that soon the entire affair resembled a mob scene from a silent movie comedy. Cooper would laugh, the Marines and the villagers would howl, the cooks would shout, the gunny would swear, and the children would giggle and eat.

For a week, the gunny fought his private war. "I've trained plenty of Marines," he would growl, "and these little imps <u>will</u> square away." In the end he was successful and the Vietnamese chow line succumbed to Marine discipline. The children got into line under the watchful eyes of their parents. But the Marines were vaguely disappointed; they had enjoyed the entertainment.

The gunny had an easier time enforcing police calls. When the children saw the Marines picking up each scrap of paper and empty tin cans, they too joined in. The project spread from the perimeter to the adjoining trails, which were widened and swept clean. Not to be outdone, the villagers spruced up their backyards, picking them clean of twigs and leaves.

The Vietnamese Popular Forces ventured farther and farther from their fortified hill. For the first time, they came forth at night. Their commander checked with Cooper each day and gradually assumed some responsibility for patrols and ambushes. His soldiers gained confidence and visited freely around the village.

The hamlet chief moved from the ARVN fort back into his own home. He arrived each day at the Marines' "social" meal, accompanied by the village elders. With dignity and just a touch of aloofness, they would pass through the crowd of villagers on the outside of the barbed wire and enter the chow line with the Marines. Occasionally, they would bring guests and make a great show of standing beside Cooper. The Marine company commander would respond by offering each a cigar and bending down to light it. The council of elders regained prestige in the hamlet of Thanh My Trung.

Cooperation followed friendship. The hamlet chief showed the Marines the favorite ambush and hiding places of the Viet Cong. One day he came running to Cooper, followed by a trembling Viet farmer. Through Piatetsky's patient questioning, Cooper learned that a squad of Viet Cong had captured the farmer while he was fishing at a nearby stream. They had taken him into the mountains and questioned him intensively about the Marines: how many they were, what they were doing in the hamlet, how long they intended to stay. They said they would kill him if he told the Marines. Once freed, he went to the hamlet chief and asked to talk with the Marine commander.

The farmer pointed to a rock outcropping on a mountain slope two miles from the hamlet. He said he was held there overnight. Cooper knew the enemy had probably left the area hours earlier. But it was obvious these Vietnamese needed reassurance of Marine protection and power.

He took the farmer and the hamlet chief to his mortar emplacement. He asked the farmer to point to the rocks. The farmer did so. Two 81mm mortars and a 106mm recoilless rifle fired at the target and the rocks were splintered apart. The farmer and the hamlet chief looked at each other and grinned.

Gunnery Sergeant Jack Montera of E/2/5 shepherds his chow line of Vietnamese children from Thanh My Trung village. (Author's photo.)

Cooper then brought the two Vietnamese to a nearby hillside where one of his platoons was firing its biweekly familiarization course. From the array of weapons, he chose a 12-gauge shotgun and a LAAW and handed them to his guests to fire. When the Vietnamese later returned to their hamlet, they walked, not like timid, frightened men, but with distinct swaggers.

Cooper didn't trust easily. He decided to see if the villagers were playing a two-sided game. Deliberately, he spread a false rumor that the Marines were leaving the next day. The next morning a Marine walking alone down the main trail was stopped by two girls who warned him that it was not safe because the VC were coming. Other Marines strolling in pairs or alone were given similar warnings. Cooper was satisfied. He had found out two things. The Viet Cong still had informers within the hamlet. But the loyalty of most villagers lay with the Marines.

Less than a month after their arrival, the Marines did leave to go on an operation. They left the marks of their influence behind in the village and especially in the hamlet. The Vietnamese had reopened two schools and a pagoda. They were washing. Their medical ills had been treated. A Vietnamese public health nurse and two school teachers had come to the village. The hamlet and village chiefs had returned. The Popular Forces were acting more like disciplined troops.

What would happen in the future, Cooper was not about to guess. But he was proud of what his Marines had done. They had worked and rebuilt the life of a hamlet. They had not thought in those terms precisely when they came. But by protecting the hamlet and patrolling the village, by example and discipline, by generosity and spirit, they had infused the will and desire for progress into a hamlet and had protected a village. Not much when compared to the millions of Vietnamese under VC control, perhaps, but more meaningful than sitting on a hill.

A HOT WALK IN THE SUN

<u>Preface</u>: On 6 August 1966, the 5th Marines launched Operation COLORADO, landing in company strength at several sites deep in Viet Cong territory, some 12 miles northwest of Chulai. Although thousands of the enemy were supposedly in the area, the companies initially met little resistance. Their search and destroy missions became what the infantrymen have termed "walks in the sun." The author describes here two such walks by two units he knew well and worked with for several weeks.

The men of Hotel Company, 2/5, moved down the road in helmets and flak jackets, weighted with ammunition and gear. They had expected a fight in this flat, populated area, so long held by the Viet Cong. They found nothing but deserted houses and warning signs scrawled on boards which formed archways above the main trail. "Marines--do not use noxious chemicals." "Death follows you here every step of the way." "Stop killing defenseless women and innocent children--protest the war." "250 members of the French Expeditionary Force are buried here--do not join them."

The Viet Cong had fled before the waves of helicopters had landed. The villagers were hiding in small caves near their homes. The Marines searched some of them. Inside one they found buried a rusty shotgun and a new carbine with hundreds of cartridges. From another they dragged two Viet Cong. One cowered and meekly obeyed the orders of his captors. The other, a well built Vietnamese in his thirties, scowled and showed no fear. The Marines would send them to the interrogator-translator team at division headquarters when they returned to base.

They did not have time to search all the caves, so they poked only into those they most suspected. A corporal heard whispering from the entrance to one large cave and Marines were stationed at both exits. The Vietnamese interpreter with the rifle company yelled into the cave. No response. A Marine threw in a smoke grenade. A dozen women and children slowly came out. They looked fearfully at the grim faces of the Marines. The Marines ignored them. The interpreter pushed them to one side.

"Is that all?" the company gunnery sergeant, Donald Constande, asked.

"No, here come the men," a corporal answered.

Two men came out. One walked directly to the waiting group of women. The other looked at the Marines, then at the interpreter, stopped, turned, and reentered the cave. Seconds later, he ran out, moving with the speed of a sprinter. He was by the infantrymen and into the jungle before anyone reacted.

Then two automatic rifles were fired at the same time. Two more rifles joined in. The firing lasted less than 10 seconds. An acrid cloud of cordite hung in the humid air in front of the cave. Bushes and small banana trees in front of the Marines were shredded.

Two Marines advanced forward. They passed from sight in the green foliage and reappeared shortly.

"He's dead," one said.

"Nothing on him. No ID card, no papers, no nothing," the other added.

"Stupid trick he pulled, huh?"

"What do you mean--stupid?" yelled the gunnery sergeant. "You're the ones that are stupid. He almost made it."

"Well hell, gunny," a Marine replied, "I've never seen a VC that close before. I didn't think he'd try to get a hat."

"Look, you just stop thinking, O.K.?" the gunny said.

The interpreter questioned the villagers. No, there were no VC in the village. They had all gone. Yes, the dead man was a VC but he thought he would be safe until he saw the interpreter. No, they didn't know who he was.

The column moved slowly forward. The villagers went back toward their houses. Nobody approached the body.

From another cave came noises.

"Now don't get trigger-happy," the gunny said, "it's probably only villagers. Just be careful. Is that clear?"

The people in the cave refused to come out. The interpreter screamed at them. They came out.

"Check it."

"O.K., gunny," a small Marine answered.

The Marine stripped to the waist and crawled into the mouth of the cave, grasping a flashlight in one hand and a .45 caliber pistol in the other. The Marines waiting heard him swear and shout angrily. There were sounds of a scuffle and he reemerged, pulling a Vietnamese by the hair.

It was an attractive young girl, sopping wet and trembling.

"She was lying in a pool of water with only her head showing," the small Marine said. "She didn't hardly want to come out."

Her white blouse was rust colored on one side.

"Check her out, doc."

The corpsman examined and treated the wounds.

"Just light shrapnel. No big thing."

"Skipper says we're behind schedule and holding up the whole show, sergeant."

"Move it out," Staff Sergeant John Wysomirski shouted to his platoon.

The fire team at point did not go thirty meters before firing broke out on the left flank. A Marine had seen six Viet Cong carrying rifles run across a rice paddy. He fired, felling one of the enemy. Two other Viet Cong had dragged the body into the concealment of a tree line.

"Let's go after them, Sergeant Ski," the Marine shouted. "I could follow their trail easy."

"Skipper says no time," the sergeant replied. "We have to find and secure a landing zone. Choppers due in an hour."

The Marines continued along the trail. It was noon and the sun was burning. There was no breeze. The helmets and the flak jackets and the heavy packs pushed down the Marines. The rifle barrels were too hot to touch. Canteens were emptied. Some men stopped sweating. Some became dizzy and chilled. Five men fell out.

Their squad leaders were furious with them. The NCOs had strongly advised their men to drink as much water as they could, especially the day and night before leaving on the operation. During each break on the march, the corpsmen had reminded the men to take salt pills. Those who wilted under the strong sun had swallowed few salt pills. Not one of them had drunk much water the previous day. They had to be carried to a landing zone. The company lost over an hour attending to the heat cases--time which could have been spent trailing the Viet Cong or conducting a more thorough search.

A ploughed-over field was selected for a landing zone and a search of the hut next to the field uncovered some war supplies--a bunch of khaki uniforms, a large medicine kit, and documents written in Vietnamese and Russian. The hut was burned and the supplies kept for processing by division intelligence.

The helicopters came and flew the company to another objective. The Marines landed in wet rice paddies and slogged toward the tree lines complaining of their fate. They encountered no enemy fire.

The company set out to find a defensive position large enough to hold the entire battalion. The Marines were entering a hamlet with a dozen houses when it began to rain. The men were elated. They stood dripping in the downpour and grinned. They emptied the iodine-treated water from their canteens and refilled them with rain water. They drank greedily.

The rain continued. A cool wind was blowing strongly and the men became chilled. The company commander, Captain Richard Hughes, told them to rent shelter in the village for the night.

"Just be grateful it ain't snowing," the gunny said.

A young man approached Hughes and through the interpreter he told his story. He said the VC controlled the valley. He had escaped from their forced labor camp in the hills. He wished to go with the Marines when they left, and take his family with him. The company commander agreed.

In late afternoon, the other companies arrived and Lieutenant Colonel Walter Moore had his men dig in for the night. Hughes asked him if they might call a helicopter in the morning to take out a few refugees."

"Sure," said the colonel, "we'll be glad to help. Anyone else, or just his family?"

Hughes said he didn't know the exact number but that the man had mentioned a few friends might want to go along.

The next day, 697 refugees were evacuated. "That guy," one Marines said, "was the greatest con artist since W. C. Fields." The Marines were stunned by the number of refugees and their determination to leave.

They came by family groups, each person carrying clumsy bundles. Some took pigs and chickens, others dogs. They asked the Marines to shoot their water buffalo and burn their homes. They said they wanted to leave nothing for the Viet Cong.

The Marines had no idea where so many people had come from, let alone how they had learned the Marines would help them.

The battalion commander requested an emergency rerouting of all available helicopters to transport the Vietnamese. All day the pilots flew the villagers from the valley to a refugee camp at Tam Ky, near the coast.

Lieutenant Colonel Moore said: "It was the damndest thing I ever saw. We came to fight VC and ended up playing Santa Claus. But you know something? We felt pretty good about it."

The Vietnamese straggled into the Marine perimeter from the east and west. Caught in the press of milling crowds and frightened by the racket of the helicopters, many children cowered and hung back. Pigs and chickens broke loose from their bonds and ran aimlessly around the landing zone.

The bearded infantrymen in soggy clothes took a proprietary interest in the Vietnamese. Those not assigned to security on the perimeter drifted toward the main trail. They stood in small groups, leaning on their rifles and watching the exodus. They drifted toward the landing zone and started helping the Vietnamese. They performed menial and kindly acts with detached and bored expressions on their faces, anxious not to attract the attention and jibes of their buddies.

Trying to cross the sopping rice paddies, an old lady floundered to a halt. Her body sagged and she dropped her meager bundle into the water. A large Marine said, "Ah, what the hell," and splashed into the paddy. He brusquely picked up the old woman and her bundle and strode toward a helicopter. Other Marines hooted and yelled at him--but without rancor. He just grinned and strode on.

A group of Vietnamese shuffled down the trail, weaving and stumbling as they carried an old man on a wooden door. They stopped to rest--the old man groaned and whimpered in a wheezing voice. Two Marines walked forward, picked up the litter, and carried the man to the landing zone.

One woman left the huddle of villagers and walked back down the trail. "Where the hell is she going?" shouted the battalion intelligence officer, Captain Richard Hemenez. "Kim, find out why she's leaving." The interpreter stopped the woman and questioned her. She replied in a shrill and angry voice. "She says her pig is not here, so she not go," the interpreter said, after five minutes of excited talk.

"Oh, for God's sake, we can't have a refugee from the refugee program. Big Moo Moo would chew my butt royally. Pass

Some of the hundreds of civilian refugees evacuated by helicopter from VC territory during Operation COLORADO are watched by Marines of 2/5. (USMC A369394)

the word to spread out and find a runaway pig."

Laughing, the Marines shouted the order down the lines. Minutes later, the unmistakable squeal of a frightened pig was heard over the clatter of the helicopters. A Marine walked along a paddy dike toward the complaining woman and the S-2 officer. In his right hand he carried his rifle; in his left hand he grasped a small screaming pig by its rear legs. The woman greeted the pig as if it were her child and returned to the group of refugees. The S-2 officer shook his head and walked away.

By late afternoon, the last Vietnamese family was evacuated. Hotel Company flew to another objective.

Three days later, Gunnery Sergeant Constande and Staff Sergeant Wysomirski were killed in action.

That same day (7 August 1966), the 1st Battalion of the 5th Marines dropped by helicopters into assigned objectives. Their area of operations lay some 3,000 meters to the east of the valley where the 2d Battalion was evacuating refugees. Charlie Company was helilifted into a small valley hit the previous night by a B-52 strike.

As usual, the zone was hit by air and artillery strikes before the 160-man company landed. The helicopters whirled down and the Marines jumped into the waist-deep rice paddies and waded toward the surrounding tree lines, staying in their heliteams. Once out of the paddies, the platoon sergeants sorted out their respective platoons, while the platoon commanders oriented themselves on their maps, not an easy process with a scale of 1:50,000. The company was twisted around the paddies in a jagged circle.

The Marines had set in a tight defensive perimeter in less than three minutes. The procedure they followed was well established; they had done it dozens of times, and, like most other times, this time they had encountered no resistance.

"Hell," growled one Marine, "it's just going to be another hot walk in the sun."

First Lieutenant Marshall (Buck) Darling studied his map carefully. Satisfied he had located his position exactly, he reported by radio to battalion headquarters and called a meeting of his platoon commanders. The company would sweep east up the mile-long valley with a platoon on either side of the main trail and one in reserve. He gave the first platoon two scout dog teams and kept an engineer attachment with company headquarters.

Before the company could move, the engineers had to destroy two boobytraps on the trail at the edge of the landing zone. Both traps had been plainly marked to warn the villagers and the markers (three bamboo poles placed around the mines in a triangular fashion) were still in place when the Marines arrived. One was an explosive charge buried under a pile of loose earth--the other a scooped-out section of the trail studded with bamboo stakes and cleverly camouflaged. With demolitions, the engineers quickly disposed of both obstacles.

First Lieutenant Arthur Blades attached a scout dog and handler team to both his first and second squads. The platoon moved forward to search the scattered huts. The area was poor. Most dwellings were small, one room huts with hard-dirt floors, mud and bamboo walls, and straw roofs. Nearly all contained deep bomb shelters. From past experience, the Marines knew chances were slight that enemy soldiers would hide in those holes. When Marines were on large offensive operations, the VC, unless cornered, fled rather than fought. Only stragglers would go to ground in exposed areas. The German Shepherd dogs enabled the Marines to move swiftly. The villagers rarely emerged from their hiding places when the Marines or even the interpreter yelled at them. But one low growl worked wonders. Cave after cave was emptied in seconds. Still the search yielded nothing--only frightened women and children.

Blades and his platoon were disappointed. They were spoiling for a fight and thoroughly exasperated with the situation. Nevertheless, the platoon commander did not allow his private opinions to influence his tactical decisions. Throughout the long and empty afternoon he yelled at his squad leaders to keep contact with each other, scolded his troops for bunching up, and insisted his flankers beat through the undergrowth and not drift into a single column. The sun sapped the Marines and gradually the pace slackened. After a few hours the dogs showed signs of fatigue and overheating. Blades prodded his men to stay alert. To an observer, he pointed out with particular pride the leadership his squad leaders were showing.

"Look at them," he said, "two are lance corporals and one just made corporal. But I wouldn't want anybody else. They know their people and work hard. They're real hardnoses."

In the third hour of the search, the Marines found a house hidden in a tree grove which contained VC khaki uniforms, medical supplies, and U.S. water cans. The material judged of intelligence value was saved; the rest, as well as the house, was burned.

In the late afternoon, Darling reported to battalion that the valley contained no enemy force. He requested a helicopter pickup. Battalion concurred.

While waiting, the Marines sat down and cooked C-rations. Few felt hungry enough to eat hot canned meat under a hot sun. In small huddles, the Vietnamese children had edged forward to peep at the Marines. A rifleman enticed one little boy to overcome his fear and venture forward to gulp a mouthful of food. Other children followed suit, timidly at first, then with gathering confidence. For the last hour the troops were in the valley, they played with and fed the children.

The helicopters came in and the Marines walked out into the rice paddies to board them.

"You know," Blades commented as he led his platoon to the landing zone, "I've been in this country for 30 days and I've never heard a shot fired in anger. I'm beginning to wonder if there really is an enemy here at all."

The children waved goodby shyly. The adults stood and watched without expression or movement. Charlie Company flew to another objective.

Three days later, they found their fight, a savage, slugging encounter which made them wonder if they would ever again gripe about a lack of action.

"GENERAL, WE KILLED THEM"

Preface: At dawn on 11 August 1966, the author arrived by helicopter in 1/5's perimeter, some 20 miles northwest of Chulai and 6 miles west of Tam Ky, a district headquarters near the South China Sea. On that perimeter 10 hours earlier, the battalion had fought the only major battle of Operation COLORADO. The author was well acquainted with the officers and men of the battalion and so, gathering in large groups, they told him in detail what had occurred and pointed out the exact positions they had held. He wrote the somber aftermath from personal observation.

I

ENCOUNTER FOR ALPHA COMPANY

After his companies, searching separately for the elusive enemy during the first few days of Operation COLORADO, had met no hard resistance, Lieutenant Colonel Hal L. Coffman had consolidated his 583-man battalion (1/5) and was sweeping toward the sea, some seven miles to the east. For three consecutive days, the route of the battalion lay along a dirt road which wound through valleys out of the foothills of scrub-covered mountains and east across monotonous expanses of flat land stretching to the sea in an unbroken succession of rice paddies, tree lines, and hamlets. The troops had uncovered little evidence to indicate the presence of a large enemy force, but each day it seemed they saw fewer villagers, while the intensity of sniper fire increased.

On the morning of 10 August, the enemy snipers were unusually persistent. All three rifle companies--Alpha, Bravo, and Charlie--encountered small groups of snipers every few hundred meters along the route of march. Enemy snipers in Vietnam are like hornets. If ignored entirely, they can sting. But if reaction is swift and aggressive, they can be swatted aside. Responding aggressively, the Marines poured out a large volume of fire each time they were fired upon. The snipers, however, carefully kept their distance, rarely firing at ranges closer than 500 yards. (The previous day a few North Vietnamese had waited until the Marine point squad was within 200 meters before firing. Those enemy soldiers had been pinned down, enveloped, and dispatched.)

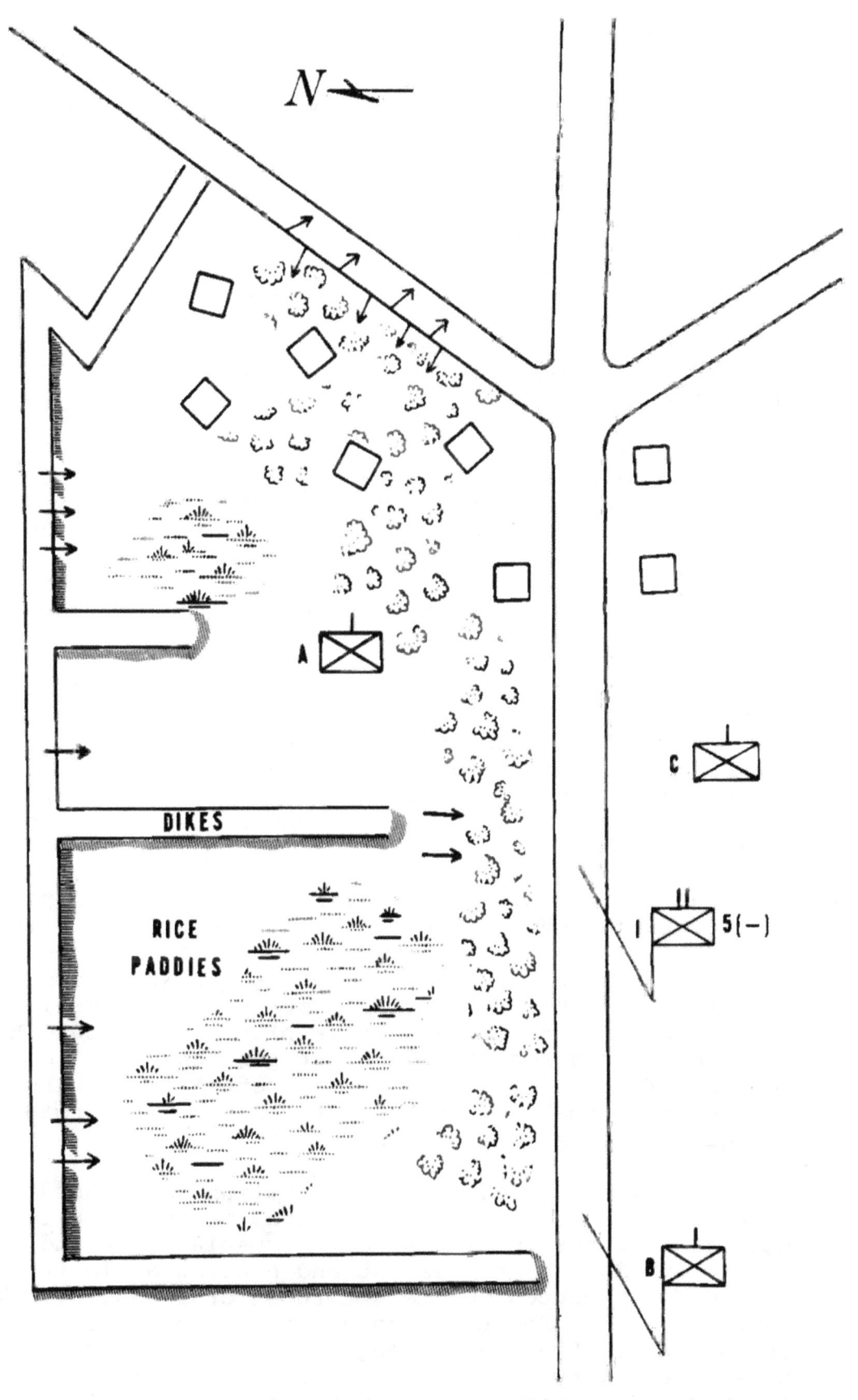

SCHEMATIC SKETCH TO ACCOMPANY "GENERAL, WE KILLED THEM"

Coffman and his company commanders did not like the situation; the troops were expending ammunition at a rapid rate with no telling effect upon the enemy. Toward noon, they ordered the squad leaders to supervise very selective return of fire in order to conserve rounds. Marching under a clear sky and searing sun, Coffman knew the helicopters could resupply his battalion but disliked making that request if not solidly engaged.

At approximately 1100, the battalion arrived at the hamlet of Ky Phu. Coffman called a halt and the men settled down in what shade they could find and began opening C rations. Shortly thereafter, word was received for 1/5 to remain in position pending the arrival of the regimental commander, Colonel Charles A. Widdecke.

After a conference with Colonel Widdecke, Coffman issued the order to push forward again. At 1400, the battalion resumed the march with the hamlet of Thon Bay as its objective. All indications were that the battalion would reach Thon Bay about 1600. Coffman liked to allow himself ample time to set in before dark. It took a few hours to tie in the lines of a battalion properly and on previous days he had allowed several hours for the task.

As they had on previous days, the companies guided on the main road which led to the sea. In front of the Marines lay acres of rice paddies gridded by thick tree lines and tangles of scrub brush, familiar enough landscapes. Groves of palm trees and patches of wooden huts dotted the roadside. Storm clouds were billowing over the mountains to the west behind the Marines.

Charlie and Alpha Companies, forming a dual point, struck off together, covering respectively the right and left flanks of the road. Both companies spread out far across the paddies. In trace along the road followed the battalion command group, consisting of the 81mm mortar platoon, the battalion headquarters, the 106mm recoilless rifle platoon (without their antitank guns), the logistics support personnel, and others. Bravo Company brought up the rear. The battalion was thus spread in a wide "Y" formation, the stem anchored on the road and the prongs pushed well out in the paddies.

Upon resuming a march, a battalion commander can generally expect a time lag of several minutes caused by a few false starts as squads, platoons, and companies jerk and bump along before sorting themselves out and hitting a smooth, steady pace. This did not happen on the afternoon of 10 August. The battalion moved swiftly. The platoons at point fanned out on both sides of the road. Slogging through paddies and twisting through tree lines, they covered more than a mile in the first 20 minutes. Rain was washing away their sweat and impeding their vision when they arrived at the outskirts of the tiny hamlet of Cam Khe at 1510. They noticed that the huts they passed were empty. Nor were there any farmers working in the rice paddies. Giving cursory glances into dugout shelters and caves, the Marines saw that they were packed with villagers.

Because of this fact, the men were alert and wary when they passed through and around the hamlet. As the 2d Platoon, Alpha Company, pushed through the scrub growth on the left flank of the hamlet, the men saw to their front a group of about 30 enemy soldiers cutting across a paddy from left to right. The platoon reacted instinctively. The men did not wait to be told what to do. Throwing their rifles to their shoulders, they immediately cut down on the enemy. Their initial burst of fire was low, short, and furious. Caught in the open, moving awkwardly through the water and slime, the enemy could not escape. Shooting from a distance of less than 150 yards, the 2d Platoon wiped them out in seconds. Farther back in the column, men thought a squad was just returning fire on a sniper. Although they did not yet know it, the battle which the Marines had sought was joined. The Marines had struck the first blow, and it had hurt.

The North Vietnamese, however, counterpunched hard. From a small hedgerow behind the fallen enemy, several semiautomatic weapons opened up and rounds cracked by high over the Marines' heads. The troops were now keyed for battle. Excited and stirred by their swift, sharp success, the platoon shifted its direction of advance and splashed into the paddy. The volume of enemy fire increased and bullets spouted in the water around the Marines. The platoon's momentum slowed as the Marines started flopping down into the water to avoid the fire. But no one had yet been hit, and the platoon quickly built up a base of fire and continued the movement by short individual rushes.

The company commander, Captain Jim Furleigh, came up, bringing with him the 1st Platoon. That unit in turn rushed into the paddy on the left flank of the 2d Platoon. The volume of enemy fire was swelling. With 70 bulky, slow-moving targets to hit at close ranges, the enemy gunners improved their air as well.

Almost in the same second, a man in each platoon was struck by machine gun bullets. Other Marines stopped firing to help the wounded men or merely to look. The rate of outgoing fire dropped appreciably. Encouraged by this, the North Vietnamese redoubled their rate of fire. No longer forced to duck low themselves, they aimed more carefully and bullets hit more Marines lying in the water. The machine gun in the tree line in front of the 2d Platoon chattered insistently, traversing back and forth in low, sweeping bursts over the Marines' heads. Two more Marines were hit. The men ducked low and, not wishing to expose themselves, fired even less in return. The attack had bogged down.

The 2d Platoon had advanced 40 meters across the paddy; the 1st Platoon not more than 20. In the tree line 100 meters away, they could see the North Vietnamese moving into better firing positions, most wearing camouflaged helmets and some clad in flak vests. The Marines could find no cover or concealment in the paddies and time was running against them. The machine gun had them pinned; the rain and mud and their heavy gear prohibited a quick, wild, surging assault. Furleigh, a sharp-eyed, quick-minded West Point graduate, assessed the situation. As he saw it, there were two alternatives: to go forward or back. What he would not do was let the company stay where it was. He thought if he urged the men, they would go forward by bounds again until they carried the enemy tree line. But casualties from a frontal assault against the effective machine gun emplacement would be heavy. Even as he pondered the dilemma, three more of his men were hit. That clinched it for him. He decided to pull back; at least that way he thought his people would escape the heavy fire and there would be time for the situation to clear and battalion to issue specific orders.

What Furleigh did not realize at that particular moment was that heavy fighting was raging in half a dozen other places, including the battalion headquarters. While Company A was attacking in the paddy, mortar shells had fallen along the road, just missing the battalion command group. The headquarters element, quite distinguishable with its fence of radio antennas, had hastily sought the concealment of the bushes and houses to the left of the road. The NCOs yelled at their sections to disperse yet stay close, and the radio operators tried to copy incoming messages and transmit at the same time. The officers were busy trying to pinpoint their position and decide on a course of action, when everyone was taken under small arms fire coming from all directions. Reports filtered in by runner and radio that Alpha Company to the northeast was pinned down and withdrawing and that to the west, at the rear of the battalion, Bravo Company was battling. To the east, on the right side of the road, Charlie Company reported it too was engaged.

In that situation, the battalion commander could not determine precisely the size or the nature of the engagement. No one could. (It probably would have been of some solace to Coffman if he had known then, as he did later, that the enemy were also caught off balance by the sudden engagement.) The headquarters group was busy defending itself. It was teeming rain in such heavy sheets that at times figures only yards away were blotted out. The visibility ceiling for aircraft had dropped to 50 feet, so no jet or helicopter support was available.

Coffman stayed calm. His was a seasoned battalion which he had commanded for 12 months. He knew his company commanders well. Faced with a battle which denied tight central control, he let his junior officers direct the fighting while he concentrated on consolidating the battalion perimeter as a whole and shifting forces as the need arose.

The situation was terribly confused. Although the battalion was on the defensive, the individual units were on the offensive. Platoons from each company were attacking separate enemy fortified positions. Caught in an ambush pushing at his left flank, Coffman wanted to draw the battalion in tight. In attempting to consolidate, the companies had to fight through enemy groups. To relieve pressure on units particularly hard pressed, Marines not personally under fire moved to envelop the flanks of the North Vietnamese. The extraction of wounded comrades from the fields of fire--a tradition more sacred than life--was accomplished best by destroying the North Vietnamese positions which covered the casualties. So isolated were the fragments of the fight that each action is best described as it happened--as a separate event. Fitted together, these pieces form the total picture of a good, simple plan which was aggressively executed, with instances of brilliant tactical maneuvers occurring at crucial moments.

By reason of extremity, Furleigh's Alpha Company played the key role in the fight during the initial hour. From the very beginning, they were in the thick of it. Private First Class Larry Baily, a mortarman assigned to company headquarters, had moved up with his company commander. The way he described it: "The VC were everywhere. They were in the banana trees; they were behind the hedgerows, in the trenches, behind the dikes, and in the rice paddies." Pulling back out of the paddy had not proved easy. Several Marines had been wounded, and one more killed, bringing to a total of five the number of American dead in the paddy. Displaying excellent fire discipline, the North Vietnamese singled out targets and concentrated a score of weapons on one man at a time. That unified enemy fire altered the exposed positions of some Marines from dangerous to doomed. Those already rendered immobile by wounds were most vulnerable to sustained sniping. These casualties (among them Baily) had to be immediately moved from the beaten zone of the bullets.

It was an arduous movement. No man could stand erect in that storm of steel and survive. So the wounded were dragged along through the flooded paddies by their comrades, much like an exhausted swimmer is towed through the water by a lifeguard. Those not dragging or being dragged returned fire at the enemy. No one later felt that fire had inflicted more than one or two casualties on the enemy. But it was delivered in unslacking volume and that disconcerted the enemy gunners and forced them to snapshoot hurriedly. Had the platoons not reestablished a steady stream of return fire, it is doubtful they could have extricated themselves, keeping their squads and fire teams intact and taking their wounded with them. By repeated exhortations, curses, and orders, Furleigh provided the guidance necessary to steady the men and prevent any slackening of fire in the moments of confusion.

Once the two platoons had reached the hedgerow, they spread out to form a horseshoe perimeter with the 1st Platoon to the left of the 2d Platoon. The open end of the horseshoe faced southwest (toward the battalion command group), and the closed end faced the enemy to the north. Furleigh tried to call artillery fire down on the enemy. In the full fury of the thunder-and-lightning storm, the adjusting rounds could not be seen or heard. Nor did anyone in Alpha Company have a clear idea where the front lines of the other companies were. For fear of hitting friendly troops, Furleigh cancelled the mission after the first adjusting rounds had gone astray.

Conspicuously absent from the battle at this crescendo was the mighty fire power of supporting weapons, proclaimed by some critics as the saving factor for Americans in encounters with the enemy. The North Vietnamese had numerical and fire superiority. Initially, it was they who freely employed supporting arms, namely mortars and recoilless rifles. What had developed for Alpha Company--and for the battalion--was a test of its riflemen.

They responded magnificently. Once tied in, the two platoons of Alpha Company needed no urging to keep fire on the enemy. At first there was an abundance of targets to shoot at, since the North Vietnamese kept leaping up and darting about from position to position. The Marines, lying prone and partially concealed in the undergrowth, put out a withering fire. They could see enemy soldiers, when hit, jerk, spin, and fall. The men shouted back and forth, identifying targets and exclaiming at their hits. They were getting back for their frustration in the paddy.

Losing in a contest of aimed marksmanship, the North Vietnamese pulled a 60mm mortar into plain view and aimed it at the opposite hedgerow. While they were popping shells down the tube, the Marines who could see the weapon were screaming: "Give us a couple of LAAWs--LAAWs up!" Several of the short fiberglass tubes were passed forward, thrown up from man to man. Some, after their long immersion in the water, failed to function. But others did and a direct hit was scored on the mortar.

While their attention was concentrated to the front, the 2d Platoon came under heavy fire from the right. So low and steady were the bursts from the automatic weapons that the platoon was unable to move against them. When the bullets came tearing in, they carried with them the sound of the weapon. Had the fire come from across the paddy, the rounds would have passed before the weapon could be heard firing. Thus, Furleigh judged there was a dug-in force within the hedgerow not over 60 meters from his right flank. He called battalion and asked that Charlie Company be committed to attack along his right flank. Coffman concurred and ordered Lieutenant Buck Darling to the assault.

Struck to earth any time they stood up, the North Vietnamese opposite Furleigh had ceased their jack-in-the-box tactics and were staying low. The machine gun which had stopped the company cold in the first attack swept wide steel swaths over the Marines' heads. Attempts to knock out the gun had been unsuccessful and had cost the company lives.

Lance Corporal R. P. Donathan had been the first to try. Donathan was lying near Furleigh when the machine gun first opened up and killed some Marines. Known throughout the battalion for his aggressive actions in fire fights, he was not cowed by the near presence of death. He asked Furleigh if he could work his way around the right flank "to get the gun." Furleigh told him to go ahead and he had set off. Several other Marines then just got up and followed him. He moved rapidly up a trail on the right of the hedgerow, his swift foray catching some enemy soldiers by surprise. These his small band cut down but the sound of the firing alerted the machine gun crew. The gun swung towards them. Caught in the open, the raiding party was at the mercy of the enemy. Behind Donathan, a Marine went down. The men on the lines heard Donathan shout, "Corpsman!"

Hospitalman 3d Class T. C. Long hurried forward. He found the wounded man lying on the trail in front of the hedgerow. While he was bandaging the man, he heard from up the trail, Donathan shout again, "Corpsman!" Long left the first casualty, having assured him he would return, and ran on. Several yards farther, he came across another Marine, hit in the leg. The casualty told him Donathan had gone on alone. Long went forward to look for him.

Both men displayed singular fortitude and determination. To go forward alone against the enemy who has struck down all others--that takes rare courage. A deliberate, conscious act of the will was made by each man when he went on alone, knowing he did not have to do so. Donathan went forward, driven by his determination to eliminate the machine gun nest. Long went forward, sensing Donathan might need him.

He worked his way carefully, bent over to present a smaller target. Occasional clusters of bullets whizzed past him. He saw a pack lying near some bushes and identified it as Donathan's. He dropped his own pack beside it and continued on, armed with a pistol and clutching his medical kit. A few yards farther on, he saw an M14 rifle and a bandolier of ammunition lying on the trail. He knew Donathan could not be far away. He looked into the bushes growing on the side of a bank next to the trail.

There was Donathan, wounded but still conscious. Long slipped down to him and began dressing the wound. He had almost finished the task when he was hit. He cried out and pitched over Donathan. Donathan sat up and reached for him.

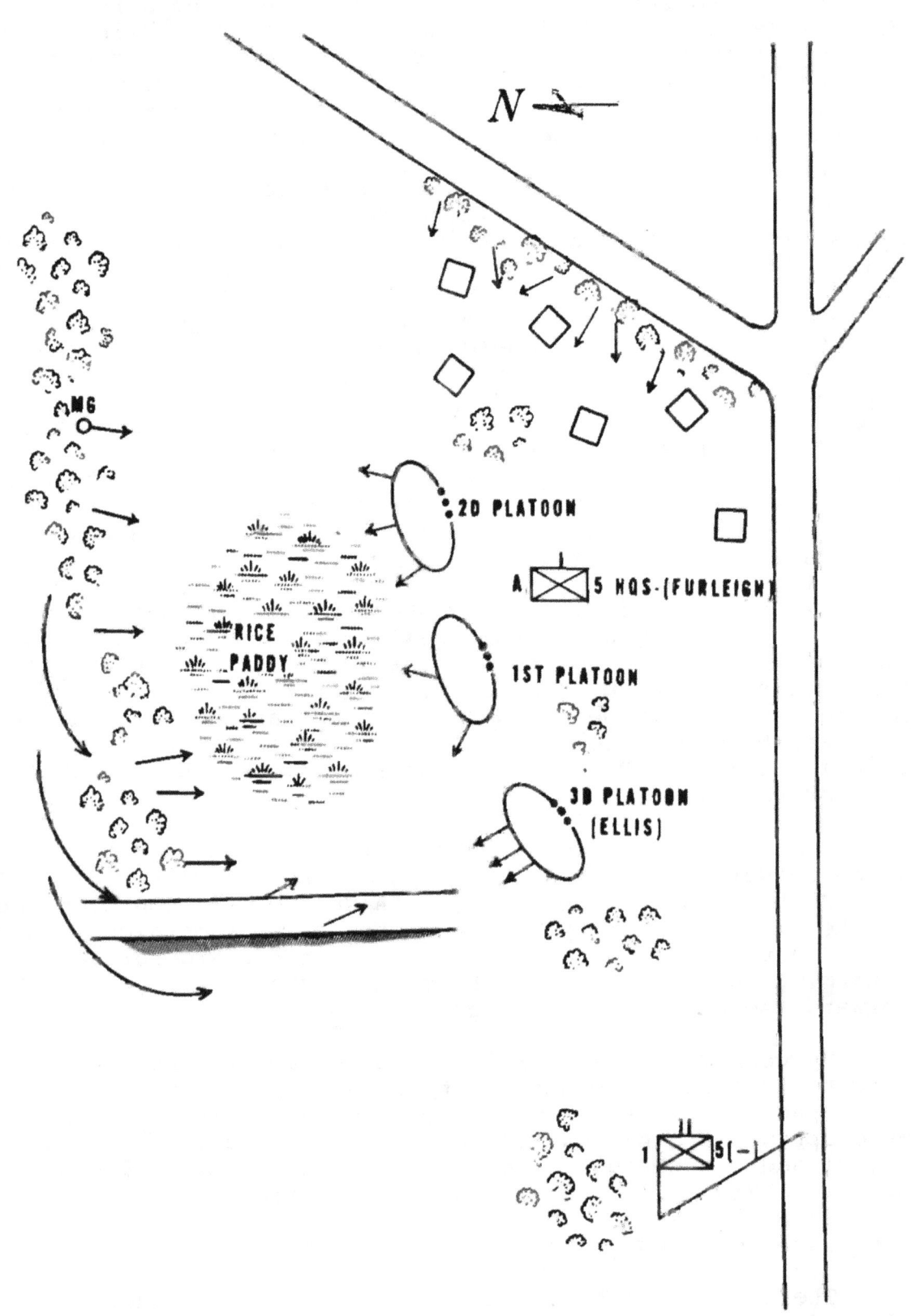

SCHEMATIC SKETCH TO ACCOMPANY "ENCOUNTER FOR ALPHA COMPANY"

"Where you hit, T. C.?", he asked.

"Back of the knee," Long replied, "the right one. Went right through--maybe shattered."

Despite his own wounds, Donathan managed to inject Long with morphine. He was trying to bandage the knee when two bullets tore into his back. He fell on top of Long, conscious but unable to move. Pinned by Donathan's weight and weak from the morphine and his wound, Long could not wiggle free. Lying in each other's arms, they talked back and forth and tried to comfort one another. It was mostly just idle talk, like many previous chatters they had in rear areas. After a while Donathan's voice just trailed off. Death claimed him quietly.

Long lay in the mud under the body with the rain pelting his face. Despite the morphine, he felt a terrible stinging in the back of his right knee. Time passed. But no one came.

It was not that they didn't try to find him. Although the trail was raked by fire, Marines crawled out by ones and twos from the hedgerow to pull back the others who had accompanied Donathan. There were five bodies sprawled in plain view of the enemy. Four were retrieved by Marines who crept through the bushes to the edge of the trail, then reached out and pulled the wounded men back into the concealment of the hedgerow. The fifth casualty, Sergeant Baker, lay in the corner of a rice paddy. Each time a Marine left the undergrowth to edge toward him, a fusillade of shots would force him back. Finally, Private First Class Robert English, a man light on his feet and agile in his movements, sprinted from the hedgerow, grabbed Baker, and ploughed back into the brush before the North Vietnamese found the range.

Furleigh then had his platoons intact and accounted for--excepting Long and Donathan. Private First Class Bielecki, the company radioman who had formerly been with the 3d Platoon, went off to look for them--a lone man in search of two lost friends. He found their packs, and the rifle and ammunition. He must have stood within 20 feet of them when he retrieved the rifle--but he did not see or hear them. He looked down into the bottom of the ditch--he might have looked right over them--but they were shielded from his view. In scrambling back to the lines, Bielecki became fatigued lugging the packs and rifle, plus his own rifle. His movements were awkward. Nevertheless, he struggled on until it suddenly occurred to him that salvaging nonessential gear under heavy fire really was not necessary or wise. He threw away the packs. Carrying two rifles, he entered the lines and reported to his company commander.

From Bielecki's report, Furleigh guessed that both Donathan and Long had been killed and their bodies dragged away by the North Vietnamese. The machine gun was still firing whenever a

Marine exposed himself. But the rain and wind had slackened and two armed Hueys whirled over the battlefield. So entangled were the battle lines that neither Furleigh nor the other company commanders were able to direct the pilots on targets. The North Vietnamese inadvertently solved the problem by firing at the helicopters, the troublesome machine gun 150 yards to Furleigh's front being one of the first enemy weapons to do so. The Hueys responded viciously, diving to pump hundreds of rounds into the tree line, turning low and tightly, and then raking the area from the opposite direction. Incoming fire on Alpha Company dropped abruptly as the enemy ducked into holes. Furleigh took full advantage of the respite to move his wounded to the battalion aid station located to his rear.

With Charlie Company driving on the right and Alpha Company holding steady to the front, the North Vietnamese began pulling their forces westward (to the left) in an attempt to outflank Furleigh and drive toward the battalion command group. The men of Alpha's 1st Platoon were becoming worried about their left flank, having seen several enemy scurrying in that direction behind the paddy dikes. Furleigh radioed to the 3d Platoon, which had been in the rear near the battalion command group skirmishing with snipers. He told the acting platoon commander, Staff Sergeant Albert J. Ellis, to bring the platoon up and refuse the left flank of the 1st Platoon.

The 37 men of the platoon moved forward to the north edge of the hedgerow. They were immediately engaged by the enemy, who were running left along a scrub-covered paddy dike 100 meters to their front. The volume of fire was intense, preventing the Marines from slipping farther right to tie in with Furleigh's group. Guided by the experience of combat, the platoon members fanned out and flopped down to form a semi-circular perimeter. They were not in visible contact with the 1st Platoon but could hear the sounds of American weapons about 60 meters to their right. To their front and left were the enemy. The 3d Platoon's fight was the Marine rifleman's dream: an engagement in which the enemy clearly showed themselves and tried to sweep the field by superior marksmanship. The 3d Platoon had waited long for the enemy to make the mistake of choosing to stand and fight. (See "No Cigar.")

With dozens of visible targets, the platoon at first ignored the basics of fire discipline and everybody just blazed away. The impact of the heavy 7.62mm bullets knocked some of the enemy completely off the dike and sent them spinning and thrashing into the paddy. The noise was deafening. The platoon commander, Sergeant Ellis, was furious. His men simply didn't have enough cartridges to expend them at a fast rate, and he doubted they would receive a resupply while the wind, rain, and lightning continued. Ellis almost went hoarse shouting, "Knock it off! Knock it off! We don't have enough ammo. You squad leaders get on your people!" Slowly the volume of outgoing fire dropped.

The platoon settled into a routine set more by reflex action than design. Made acutely aware by Ellis that they might fight indefinitely, the men, only minutes before profligate, became absolutely miserly in their use of bullets. They would fire only when a distinct target appeared, and then generally but one round per man.

The enemy, pushed to the earth, started building up their own base of fire. Soon automatic weapons were rattling all along the dike, and Marines felt the sharp blast of 60mm mortar shells slamming into their perimeter. The North Vietnamese had better cover and firing positions than the Marines. They could steady their weapons on the mud dike and expose only their heads and shoulders while firing. They had ample ammunition and outnumbered the Marines perhaps five to one. One out of every four Marines was hit in the fight (but only two were killed). The enemy used aimed fire, attested by the fact that every member of the platoon later recounted seeing the splashes of rounds hitting near him.

Near misses to Marines were common, and one was even comical. Lance Corporal Robert Matthews, a fire team leader in the 1st Squad, was firing from the prone position when a bullet hit his pack and knocked him sideways. He lay quite still, feeling a hot, sticky substance spread over his back. He yelled, "I've been hit!" Another rifleman crawled to him and gently slid off the damaged pack. Then the rifleman laughed and said: "That's not blood." Matthews' 'wound' had been caused by the bursting of a can of shaving cream.

Corporal Rodney Kohlbuss took several casualties in quick succession in his 2d Squad. He ordered his men to pick up the wounded and move to more protected positions. The men found the shift difficult, but so strong are the habits of training that they tried to take all their equipment with them. Kohlbuss yelled to them to drop the excess gear and move. This they did, while the other two squads provided covering fires.

In addition to those killed or wounded in action, Ellis had one man, Private First Class George Fudge, missing from the platoon during the first hour. When the fight first began, Fudge was walking well ahead of his platoon to keep contact with the 1st Platoon to their front. In the initial burst of firing, he thought he heard a strange sounding machine gun to his right front. The 1st Platoon seemed not to hear it, for they veered toward the swelling sounds of the fight to the left. Still thinking the point was just brushing off snipers, Fudge was reluctant to alert the 3d Platoon by voicing his suspicions. He decided instead to investigate alone the noise he had heard. Avoiding the main trail, he cut between two huts, and proceeded to pick his way carefully through a thin screen of underbrush. When he was abreast of the back yard of another house, he stopped to look and listen. He flicked an indifferent glance at the yard, studded with stumpy banana trees, and was about to proceed when he looked again in disbelief. The trees were walking. Fudge was not inexperienced. A trained sniper, he had spotted and shot several well-camouflaged Viet Cong in previous battles. But never had he seen such perfect concealment. Had the North Vietnamese not moved, he would have walked right past them and probably been shot in the back.

With their backs toward him, the North Vietnamese were clustered around a machine gun set up on a paddy dike. Fudge did not hesitate. It never occurred to him to go back and get help. Standing 50 meters from the North Vietnamese, he raised his rifle to his shoulder, sighted in carefully, and fired twice. Two of the enemy fell--the others, obviously stunned, turned and just gaped at Fudge. He fired two more times and two more enemy soldiers went down. Before he could fire again, the fifth enemy soldier reacted like a stuntman in a war movie. Pushing off from his heels, he flipped backwards over the dike in a somersault and came up blazing away with a submachine gun. That alerted other North Vietnamese that there was an enemy in the midst of their positions.

Bullets whipped by Fudge from all directions. He fell flat and lay perfectly still for a moment. He was startled by the savage, if belated, onslaught and angered that he had missed a perfect score. The unmanned machine gun attracted his attention next. He threw a grenade and it landed squarely on target. Satisfied with himself on that account, he crawled back toward his platoon, belatedly aware that the company had engaged more than a few snipers.

En route, he bumped into a party of men from the 1st Platoon moving the wounded to the rear. He joined them to help carry the poncho litters. He made several round trips, adding to his tally when an enemy soldier stepped out from behind a bush 150 meters away. Fudge dropped him with one round.

When Fudge finally rejoined the 3d Platoon, Ellis was so glad to see the deadly sharpshooter that he didn't even chew him out for being gone so long. He just sent Fudge into the fray and told him to get busy. Fudge did not disappoint his platoon commander. Before dark, his rifle brought down five more enemy.

The platoon was armed with LAAWs, grenade launchers, machine guns, and rifles. The men who had LAAWs and M79s engaged the fortified positions from which the enemy were laying down a web of cross fires. Lance Corporal Robert Goodner proved most effective with the LAAWs. With one shot he blasted an automatic weapons emplacement 150 meters away. The backblast from the recoilless weapon whipped up a gust of spray which marked his position, and, under a hail of bullets, he half-crawled, half-swam away.

Others had noted his success and he was asked to try for another gun which had a group of Marines pinned. Goodner wormed his way to a vantage point, waited until the gun fired, and sighted in. The range this time was 250 meters. The rocket hit the target squarely and pieces of the gun flew into the air.

To conserve ammunition, the machine gunners kept their bursts extremely short, but even so, with targets plentiful, the gun barrels were soon steaming. Having hastily set up, the gunners found that their fields of fire were extremely limited. Attempts to shift positions for delivery of enfilade fire were thwarted by the special attention given them by enemy gunners. The weapons squad leader, Lance Corporal Ronald Moreland, was one Marine who did not curse the rain; it kept his guns from overheating and malfunctioning.

The performance of the riflemen was a study in marksmanship. The leaders of the platoon had been known to walk the line in a fire fight urging the men to "hold them and squeeze them, hold steady and shoot low." The men had gotten over their initial desire to fire frantically and were putting out rounds one at a time, firing sparsely and carefully. Ammunition had been replenished slightly by taking the bandoliers of the casualties and redistributing them to those still firing. The Marines had a clear view of the dike. At 100 yards, the North Vietnamese were in serious trouble dueling with riflemen trained to hit a 20-inch bullseye at 500 yards.

Failing to break the Marine perimeter by frontal fire, the enemy again tried to shift their forces westward and turn the Marines' left flank. Corporal Carl Sorensen held that flank with his 3d Squad. His men shouted to him that they could see large groups of the North Vietnamese crawling and darting to their left. He passed the word to his platoon commander--Ellis told Furleigh, who in turn notified battalion. Lieutenant Colonel Coffman called Bravo Company, already fighting their way forward, and told them to get a unit up on the double to tie in the left flank of the 3d Platoon, Alpha Company.

Kohlbuss' squad exacted a terrible toll when the enemy lifted their base of fire and tried to slip past. In moving, the enemy soldiers exposed part of their bodies over the top of the dike. Every time an enemy raised up, the entire squad would fire together. They developed a rhythm to their volleys. It was like knocking down ducks in a shooting gallery. A figure would pop up behind the dike, a dozen rifles would crack, and the figure would pitch sideways and disappear from sight.

But while the battle to the front was going well for the 3d Platoon, the pressure on their left flank was increasing. More and more enemy were coming from the northeast, trying to cut wide around the platoon. The men of the 3d Squad estimated between 75 and 100 enemy soldiers were seeking to skirt around them. The platoon did not have enough ammunition to beat off a determined attack by a group that size. Ellis sent Sorenson to the left rear with instructions to find Bravo Company and guide forward a relief force.

II

THE BULLS OF BRAVO

Bravo was moving up, not without difficulty. When the fight had first begun, the company was spread out far to the rear of the battalion command group. The march order went: 1st Platoon, 2d Platoon, and 3d Platoon, with the 1st Platoon dispersed through both the paddies and the tree lines on the left flank.

The 1st Platoon ran into trouble shortly after Alpha Company became engaged. To their left flank, they saw about 40 of the enemy with bushes tied to their backs trotting north across a wide field seeking the concealment of a tree line. The platoon fanned out and gave chase. The 2d Squad surged ahead and swept through the same field the North Vietnamese had deserted. The 1st and 3d Squads were slightly to the rear and keeping to the edge of the hedgerows.

Twenty feet from the tree line, the 2d Squad was lashed by a blaze of automatic weapons fire. Trapped in the open, the squad was hard hit and men began yelling for help. Three of the nine men had been badly wounded and one killed. The Marines who could still fire did so and the sound of their weapons brought help.

The 2d Squad was lying flat in the grass and the other two squads, staying to the hedgerows to the rear, could not see them. By this time they too were under fire and being kept busy. But Sergeant Darwin R. Pilson, the right guide of the platoon, worked his way forward to the sound of the M14s. The 2d Squad had been expending rounds feverishly, trying to smother with fire an enemy machine gun and then move out of the open into the cover of the tree line. The North Vietnamese, however, had returned round for round from a deep trench and the squad had made no progress. When the Marines' fire became particularly intense, the machine gun would stop firing, only to begin a short time later from a different section of the trench. The men shot several enemy who incautiously poked their heads through the underbrush but they could not knock out the gun, which was delivering fire not a foot over their heads. When Pilson reached them, Private First Class Eugene Calogne had just killed a sniper with his last bullet.

Pilson dumped his ammunition on the ground beside them, told the squad leader, Corporal Nuncio, he would bring help, and crawled away. He reached the company headquarters and reported to the company commander, Captain Sullivan, that the squad was pinned down and had taken several casualties. He grabbed a grenade launcher and was about to set off again when Sullivan told him, "Slow up, I'll get you some help."

Sullivan now had three distinct problems to solve. In addition to the 2d Squad's predicament, he had just received word from the battalion commander to send men forward to block the left flank of Alpha Company which was in danger of being enveloped. And the company command group itself was being subjected to intense fire from a village 500 yards to their left rear.

The 1st Platoon was fighting on the flank and the 3d Platoon was guarding the rear, under fire but not pressed. That left the 2d Platoon to commit. Sullivan split the platoon, sending the 2d and 3d Squads up the road to find and help Alpha Company, while Sergeant Ronald Lee Vogel took the 1st Squad and set out to relieve Nuncio's squad.

Pilson had gone ahead, laden with ammunition and sporting for a fight. Marines engaged in a dozen places saw him go by, moving steadily into the thick of it, stopping only to fire or reload or throw a grenade. Perhaps the gods of war favored the dauntless that day, since he never got scratched though men fell on both sides of him. He reached the 2d Squad, distributed more ammunition, and joined the fray.

Vogel's squad slugged its way forward. The rain was falling in sheets and the North Vietnamese held many of the intermingled hedgerows. It was impossible to identify a man at 70 yards. Vogel lost a man before they had gone a hundred yards when a figure in utilities and a Marine helmet loomed up out of the dusk across a paddy. The squad paid him no attention until he fired and killed a Marine and ducked to the undergrowth. The slain man's friend, Lance Corporal Robert Monroe, jerked a grenade from his cartridge belt shouting, "I'm going to kill that _____." Vogel told him to keep low and stay in the hedgerow but Monroe, beside himself with fury, started to move into the open anyway. Vogel reared up and hit him, the force of the blow knocking Monroe flat. Other Marines held him fast until he calmed down and agreed to follow orders.

Vogel's men reached the field without taking any further casualties. They split up and crawled through the grass to search for the dead and wounded of the 2d Squad. None presumed to assault the trench line only a few feet away. Their orders were to recover the casualties and it was this task they set about.

But in a fascinating testimony to the thoroughness of the training they had received, the unwounded Marines of the 2d

Squad had continued the attack. Nuncio and some others had crept forward trying to penetrate the enemy lines. The grass and their closeness to the earth impeded their vision so the squad members could not see one another, yet they all moved in one direction--forward.

Vogel had to split his own squad to find them. Some men dragged the casualties back, while others inched forward listening for M14s. Monroe found Private First Class Gregory Pope lying under a bush a few yards from the tree line. Pope was in the rifleman's classic prone position, legs spread, elbows up and in, cheek resting along the stock of his rifle. So intent was his concentration that he ignored Monroe's presence at first. From the constant crackings overhead it was obvious to Monroe that the enemy was equally intent on disposing of Pope, and had a lot more firepower. Monroe, fully recovered from his irrational rage, now in turn became exasperated with Pope.

"Hey," he yelled, "what are you doing? You're all alone out here."

Startled, Pope replied, "Is that right? Then let's get the hell out of here."

Monroe wasn't exactly right, although he had no way of knowing otherwise. Three Marines had almost succeeded in storming the trench. They had reckoned that if they were able to sneak close enough, they could rush the crew of the machine gun before the enemy moved to another position. So thinking, Privates First Class Calogne, Pico, and Millian edged toward the sound of the gun, and right into its field of fire before they realized they were trapped. Pico and Millian were hit moving between two trees not over 20 feet from the trench. The trees were about 13 feet apart and were used as aiming points by the gun crew. Calogne helped the two men crawl to shelter behind the tree on the right and there the three lay, listening to the bullets fly by and pitching grenade after grenade into the trench with no noticeable effect. They had run out of grenades and were firing carefully spaced single shots when some men from Vogel's squad heard them and came up. These Marines stayed to the left of the machine gun's fire lane and protected the flank. Hospitalman 3d Class Harold Lewis reached Pico and Millian, and he and Calogne pulled them back.

This completed the extraction of the 2d Squad, a unit of resolute men.

The wounded were brought back to Bravo Company's command center, a position at that moment almost as perilous as the ones where they had been hit. It was an easy target to mark, since Marines were constantly bringing in wounded and ducking out with ammunition and instructions. The command group was

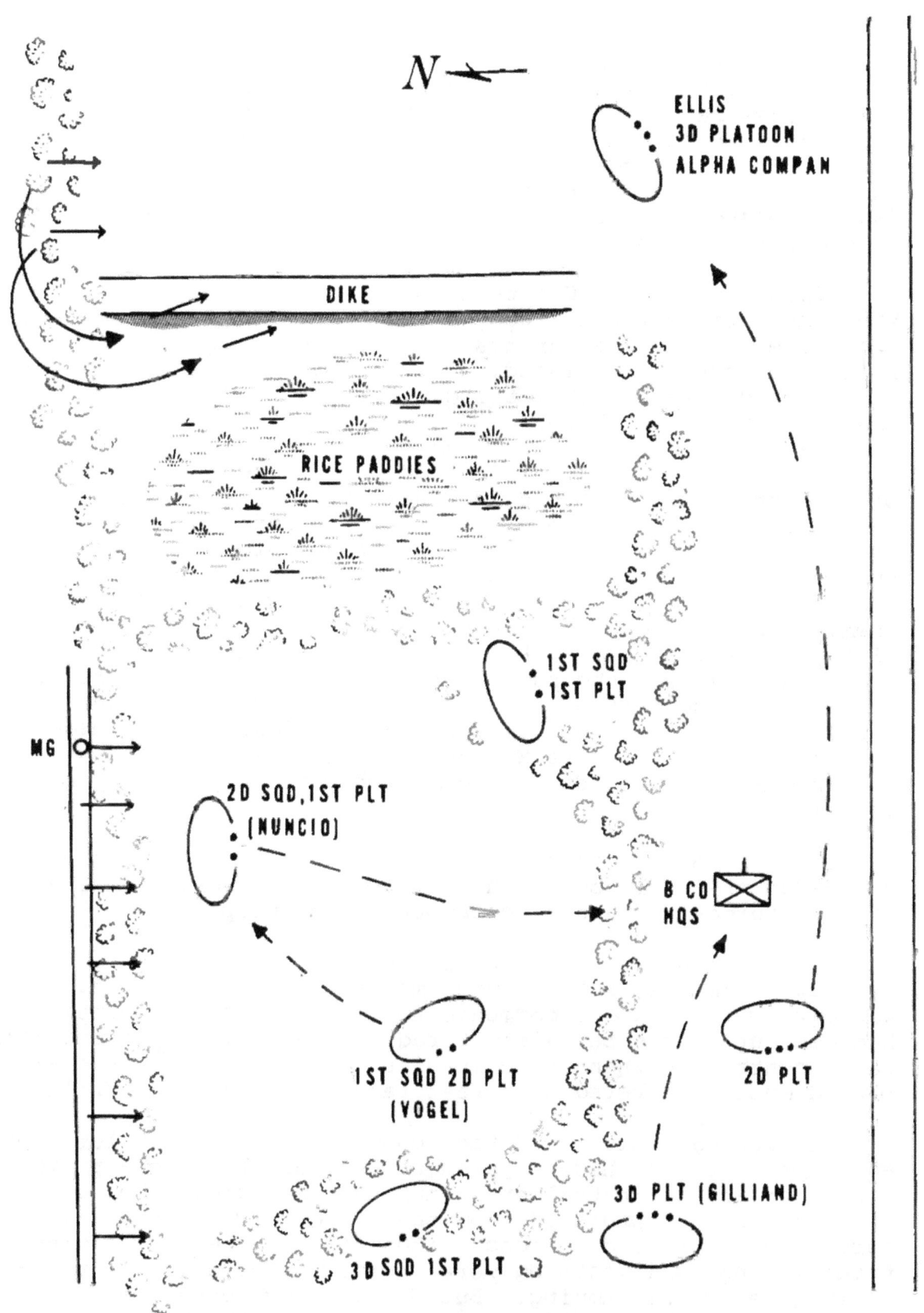

SCHEMATIC SKETCH TO ACCOMPANY "THE BULLS OF BRAVO"

always in motion, with Gunnery Sergeant Thomas Beandette, Corporal Smith, and Hospitalman 2d Class Robert Feerick sallying forth several times to bear in the wounded. Privates First Class Patrick Scullin and James Henderson wandered in, carrying a wounded Marine and a prisoner whom they had captured by knocking him unconscious. They had become separated from the machine gun section with the 2d Platoon and together had fought up and down the left flank before making contact with some other Marines.

From a village 400 meters to the northwest, the North Vietnamese brought heavy weapons to bear on the command center. They tried to hit the Marines clustered there with a 3.5-inch rocket launcher, and missed. They tried with 57mm recoilless rifles, and missed. They tried with .50 caliber machine guns and the rounds went high.

They tried with a 60mm mortar, and succeeded. They almost blew up the wounded of the 2d Squad at their moment of deliverence. The casualties were being carried across the paddy in front of the hedgerow when a mortar round plunged down behind them. The litter bearers hastened their steps and gained the concealment of the bushes just as a second shell burst behind them. Lance Corporal Van Futch, a company radio operator sitting in the hedgerow, had been watching the mortars chase the wounded across the paddy, and thought: "Uh-oh, here it comes now. The next one will be right in here." He was correct. The next shell dropped in the middle of the hedgerow and struck down two more Marines. Flak jackets were hastily thrown over the wounded as the men prepared to receive more incoming.

None came. A rifleman had located the enemy mortar pit, and Sergeant Peter Rowell quickly fired his own 60mm mortar. The countermortar fire silenced the enemy weapon.

During that exchange, Sullivan took shrapnel in the leg. It slowed him down but did not impede his effectiveness. He was more worried about communications. The North Vietnamese had come up on the battalion's radio frequency and were jamming radio contact between the companies. Over the air the enemy played music, jabbered at a fast rate, and whistled shrilly.

It worked, only the Marine communicators didn't let the enemy know it. It had happened to the battalion on a previous operation and the battalion communication officer, Captain Milt Harmon, had profited from that experience. His communicators were instructed to ignore the interference and continue transmitting as if nothing were wrong. After a while, the enemy gave up the jamming. But Sullivan was uneasy over the prospect that they could resume the tactic at any time.

And after pulling back the casualties and straightening out his left flank, he needed to contact his 3d Platoon. The 2d Platoon was fighting with Alpha Company and the men around him, from the 1st Platoon, were near exhaustion from their efforts. He had to have fresh troops to carry the wounded to the battalion evacuation point and he could use more firepower if the enemy persisted in probing a route for an envelopment.

He managed to contact the 3d Platoon commander, First Lieutenant Woody Gilliland, and that staunch individual lost no time in bulling his way forward. His platoon arrived fresh and intact. The company commander and his gunnery sergeant made no effort to hide their feelings at the sight of the ex-football player jogging towards them along the hedgerow.

"Brother, I could kiss you!" exclaimed the gunny, momentarily forgetting rank and sex.

Sullivan turned responsibility for the casualties over to Gilliland, whose platoon carried them to a rice paddy marked as a landing zone. Suitably, a landing zone must be secure--free from hostile fire--before the helicopters can land. But large, lumbering craft though the H-34 troop helicopter is, it can be surprisingly difficult to destroy, as events were to show.

It was still raining but the ceiling had risen enough for the medical evacuation helicopters to come in, provided they were not shot out of the air.

The troops on the ground tried to clear an area; it just couldn't be done. The battalion command group were still using rifles and the 106mm recoilless rifle platoon was shooting snipers out of trees. The three rifle companies were fighting tooth and nail. There was no respite. The Hueys were striking all around the perimeter. The Marines marked their lines or targets by popping smoke grenades, only to have the enemy follow suit. A Marine would pitch a yellow smoke grenade and no sooner would it billow than a half dozen clouds of yellow would filter from surrounding hedgerows. Sullivan resorted to the SOP* established for such emergencies. The troops would heave a combination of different colored grenades and the pilots would identify over the radio the color schemes. Notified when they had seen the right combination, the Hueys could bear in. Their presence suppressed enemy fire but the minute they flew off, the North Vietnamese emerged from their holes and resumed the battle. As Gilliland gathered the casualties, he knew their only chance of being flown out depended on the skill and courage of the H-34 pilots. If they came in, they would do so virtually unprotected.

---

*SOP - Standing Operating Procedure

Of the four H-34s which conducted the medical mission, two were shot down, neither over the battlefield itself, and a crew chief was killed. The first craft in, piloted by Captain Lee, had been wracked by fire. Crippled after running a gantlet of crossfires, it fluttered back to base headquarters two miles south at Tam Ky, where it sputtered out altogether. The second craft was luckier. First Lieutenant Ellis Laitala dropped his bird down to 200 feet and still could not see the nose of the helicopter. He tried twice more to find a break in the cloud cover and finally succeeded, only to run into fire. The enemy had had ample time to prepare for his arrival after he had clattered over the landing zone a few times and when he did cut through the rainy mist, they had a .30 caliber machine gun talking. Laitala's copilot, First Lieutenant Richard Moser, saw a burst of tracers zip by his right window chest-high. Turning to tell Laitala the enemy was zeroed in, he saw another burst streak by the left window.

"It's a good thing that guy didn't hold one long burst," he said.

Laitala made 10 trips to bring in ammunition and first-aid dressings and to evacuate casualties. On each approach and take-off he received fire. He put his helicopter through a series of desperate gyrations each time to shake off the streams of tracers, pitting flying skill against marksmanship.

The third pilot to land shared Lee's fate. Major Raymond Duvall's craft was hit repeatedly. During the two hours he was flying in the area, he flew through more concentrated fire than he had seen in his 11 previous months in Vietnam. Despite the intensity of that fire, Duvall refused to allow his gunners to open up. In this area, and at dusk, it was difficult to distinguish the Marine positions from those of the enemy. A wild machine gun burst, if the helicopter suddenly rocked, could kill Marines just as quickly as North Vietnamese. What finally forced him down was a hit in the rotor blade. The torn hole caused a terrible shrieking noise with every revolution of the blade and the troops on the ground were sure he would crash. But, like Lee, Duvall managed to wobble back to Tam Ky.

Among the helicopters, though, the one most memorable to Gilliland and the troops of Bravo Company was YL54. "I'll never forget that one," Gilliland said. "I don't know how he did it. He should have been nailed a dozen times."

Captain Robert J. Sheehan was flying YL54 in an exceptional manner. Ordinarily, a helicopter is travelling through the air at a speed of 80 to 90 knots when it approaches a landing zone. Sheehan hit the landing zone doing 115 knots--to a layman this difference may not seem like much but Sheehan's copilot, First Lieutenant Marshall Morris, explained:

"They had our altitude pegged. I'd say if we were going 5 knots slower, they'd have had us. Captain Sheehan really revved it up and just plain outran the tracers. It was a speed I know I couldn't do."

In a conversation later, however, Sheehan himself was quick to point out that landing an H-34 helicopter could not be a one-man show.

"It's a team effort," he said, "like a rifle squad. The crew chief checks out the side door to make sure the tail is clear of obstructions when we come in. The gunner has to suppress hostile fire. The copilot backs up the pilot at all times. The copilot doesn't grab the controls but he palms them, like with kid gloves. If the pilot is hit on landing and the copilot is daydreaming, the bird would probably crash."

On his first trip in, Sheehan picked up eight wounded and headed out south at treetop level. He flew straight into a wall of bullets, one of which hit the carburetor. Sheehan quickly pulled right and the tracers fell behind. The hostile fire was like that on each of the nine trips he made and the helicopter was struck on three separate occasions. On the second trip, his gunner, Sergeant J. B. Jensen, was hit but the round ricocheted off his thick pilot's flak jacket. Sheehan allowed his gunners to fire and he could actually see their rounds finding targets. Jensen spun two enemy soldiers completely around with one long burst of his M60 machine gun while the crew chief, Lance Corporal Baker, dropped another who was crouched in a trench.

Altogether, Sheehan flew in 2,400 pounds of ammunition and 400 pounds of battle dressings and took out 20 casualties. The last evacuation proved the most difficult. Coming in, Sheehan attracted fire from all directions. Some enemy were hidden not more than 50 yards from the helicopter, whose occupants could see the hostile positions much more clearly than could the Marines on the ground. But all the linked cartridges for the machine guns had been used up. Their plight seemed so bad Baker swung himself out the helicopter door onto the steel lift step and returned fire with a .38 pistol. A Navy corpsman named King, along to attend the casualties, saw this and said, "_____ it, I'd better get out there too."

With that, he leaned out and began to fire his .45.

Sheehan put down and the infantrymen brought up a casualty. They shouted, "Two more are coming!" Sheehan jerked his thumb up in the air to signal he understood and would wait. And wait he did, for a full five minutes while the North Vietnamese tried frantically to destroy YL54. Tracers were whining by at all angles, like a swarm of angry bees. From the village outside Sullivan's perimeter came the fire helicopter pilots hate most, that of .50 caliber machine guns speaking in tandem. The tracers rushed by in streams. Sheehan watched a paddy dike to his left front shred away. The foliage on a nearby hedgerow fell away like leaves in an October wind.

Across a paddy, a group of Marines struggled forward, half-dragging, half-lugging two wounded wrapped in ponchos. Sheehan remembered thinking it would be a good idea to carry a number of stretchers in his helicopter when he went to the assistance of Marines in the future, if there were a future for YL54. He was not going to leave without those two Marines but he thought the furious fires would reach him before they did. Gilliland shared that belief and stared at the stubborn helicopter in amazement. It sat, and was pounded by bullets in the belly, and sat some more, until the two wounded had reached it. Then Sheehan whirled away and Gilliland vowed to remember that helicopter.

Once airborne and heading south, Sheehan called over the intercom to check on his men.

"Hey," he said, "how are you guys doing back there?"

"Hell, Captain," came the cheeky reply, "we're having a ball."

The weather and the situation were clearing all around the perimeter. The Hueys were fluttering back and forth and had pinpointed the sections of the village to the left front of Bravo Company from which the heaviest concentration of hostile fire was pouring, including the .50 caliber machine guns which had unsuccessfully searched for Sheehan. One helicopter pilot, acting as the Tactical Air Controller Airborne (TACA), had the responsibility for selecting and designating targets for fixed-wing aircraft. He called down the jets, A4D attack planes specially designed for close air support. The Huey pilot could see the tracers of a .50 caliber machine gun winking from the side of a hill above the village. Captain D. T. Healy dropped down on the target, his jet ducking up and out over the village before the hill reverberated from the shock of a 2,000-pound bomb. As he levelled off, the Huey pilot informed him he had received a heavy volume of fire from the village as he went in and when he pulled out of his run. Healy had been unaware of this.

Circling above the battlefield, Healy's wingman, First Lieutenant J. F. Schneider, Jr., could see the village clearly. The TACA told him to come in. Schneider had begun his dive when the TACA radioed to him to pull out, he wanted more time to spot the exact source of the fire. He did this by flying over the village and drawing fire, a tactic not recommended for the faint of heart. Satisfied he had designated the target area properly, he told Schneider to come in again.

Schneider entered his dive doing 300 knots. He concentrated on his target--the northeast end of the village--released the 2,000 pounder and pulled out doing 450 knots.

To the men of Bravo Company who watched his dive, it had been a marvelous spectacle. In the growing dusk and gloom they had seen the jet slide down a thick red stream of tracers, then pull out, leaving behind a shattering splash of light and dirt. The infantrymen actually cheered.

In his gathering speed and steep approach angle, Schneider had been completely unaware his jet was the object of such concentrated fire. His plane had not been touched.

The recoilless rifles and .50 caliber machine guns did not speak again from the village. Following the strike, Bravo Company received only desultory sniper fire and Sullivan consolidated his lines with remarkable ease. Coffman then directed him to bring his company up the road. Help was needed in bringing out the casualties from Charlie Company, which had fought the hardest battle of all.

III

THE ASSAULT OF CHARLIE COMPANY

It was the premonition of a combat rifleman which kept Charlie Company from walking into a bad situation even before the fight had started. Charlie Company had swept east through the village on the right side of the road and arrived at a large open rice paddy bordered by thick hedgerows. There the road split, one trail angling northeast off to the left, flush against a tree line, the other running due east across a paddy, 75 meters removed from the undergrowth.

Corporal Frank Parks was leading the point squad. He was worried by the absence of the villagers and the lack of cows in the fields. He believed the company was going to be hit. While he was hesitating, a fusillade broke out to his left rear, where Alpha Company was. He thought someone had flushed a few snipers. But faced by two trails, he chose to bring the lead element of the company out across the paddy away from the hedgerow to the left. He reasoned that, if they were hit from that flank, they could take cover behind the road-dike and build up a superior volume of fire. He did not want to be hit from positions two feet away.

Parks gestured to his point man, Private First Class Tyrone Cutrer, and Cutrer parted the bushes and walked into the open. Other Marines followed and the company bore to the right, leaving the hedgerow on the left flank for Alpha Company to prod. Cutrer's platoon, the 3d, was well into the paddy when they began taking fire from the hedgerow. The rounds were passing high and didn't bother the men. The Marines estimated not more than five or six enemy were shooting at them.

Their reaction was immediate; they wheeled left and rushed the tree line. They screamed and shouted as they slogged across the paddy, a tradition which had become a habit in the company over many months and many fire fights. They could hear answering shouts and cries to the rear where the 81mm mortar platoon was marching. Between the rifle company and the heavy mortar platoon a bond of friendship had been struck and, hearing Charlie Company go into action, the mortarmen were lending them all the verbal support they could. The air was filled with rifle shots, wild shrieks, and loud cries of "Go get 'em, Charlie!" "Whomp up on those _____!", "Do some dinging, Charlie!" "Kill them dead!"

Park's point squad had a jump on the rest of the company and had almost closed on the hedgerow when a man was hit and went down. The others slowed their momentum, hesitated, then flopped down no more than 15 meters from the bushes.

This slack period while they tended to the casualty gave the North Vietnamese time to recover and build up an effective base of fire. Before the Marines could resume their push, heavy automatic weapons fire was pouring above their heads. Still, they were very close, so close that Cutrer yelled "Let's go up on the bushline!" and bounded forward the few remaining yards. He was thrown right back out by the blast of a grenade and for a few seconds stood erect in front of the bushes, deaf and dazed. Recovering his senses, he picked up the rifle which had been blasted from his hands and rushed forward again. This time he was joined by two more Marines and all three ran full into another grenade. Cutrer's luck held and he was the only one not injured. He dragged his two companions down into the shelter of a drainage ditch outside the hedgerow and put battle dressings on their wounds. Finishing that task, he picked up a grenade launcher and pumped several shells into the bushes in quick succession. Strung out along the ditch, the squad lay flat and covered the hedgerow with area fire. Their attack had been stopped cold.

First Lieutenant Buck Darling, commanding Charlie Company, later expressed dissatisfaction (as had Furleigh of Alpha Company) with the tendency of the troops at precisely the worst moment to turn aside from attacking the enemy to care for the wounded.

"Once a person gets hit," he said, "and your fire and maneuver stops in a paddy, your momentum is dead. It gives the enemy a chance to sight in. When the next man gets up, he'll get dinged*--then nobody wants to get up. So you might as well have them crawl back across the paddies. If you could get them up on a line and charge, you might carry the position--with casualties, of course. But you'll probably not get the men to do that all at once together."

"If I'd made it in that first half-hour," he added ruefully, "I'd have squeezed them up."

At about this time, Darling received a call from Lieutenant Colonel Coffman. Coffman explained that Alpha Company was being hit from a trenchline to their right flank and he wanted Darling to attack it and relieve part of the pressure on Alpha. Darling thought that Coffman must have read his mind, since that trenchline was the enemy position which had just repulsed the 3d Platoon and Darling at that precise moment was preparing to assault it in force.

Darling was a seasoned commander and a master of small-unit tactics. He had been with the battalion for 30 months, longer than any other man, and had extended his tour in Vietnam to keep his company. Unruffled by fire and at his best when actively engaged, Darling took his time to gauge the measure of the enemy which confronted him. His 3d Platoon was engaged on the left flank, his 2d had encountered no enemy on the right, and his 1st Platoon was holding fast to the rear in reserve. Before further committing his forces, Darling turned control of the company over to his executive officer, First Lieutenant Ron Benigo, and went forward to assess the situation. In this action he was motivated not by bravado but by his knowledge of close-in combat.

"A small-unit leader," he said, "in thick brush can do nothing talking over the radio. He has to go see, which means you have to leave somebody back to coordinate things while you go up to decide on a tactical maneuver."

What Darling saw prompted him to employ the classic small-unit maneuver: lay down a frontal base of fire and envelop from the flank. It is a simple, direct solution but very hard to repulse if the defenders have left the end of a flank dangling. And the North Vietnamese had done exactly that.

Darling brought up the 2d Platoon and dispersed them along the dike-road. From there they could deliver fire on the hedgerow and be protected themselves. They moved far enough out into the paddy to shoot past the right flank of the 3d Platoon and the machine gun crews set up their guns in pairs, with excellent fields of fire. Darling thus had over a hundred weapons massed to rake a tree line not 200 meters long.

---

*dinged - Marine slang for a man being wounded or killed.

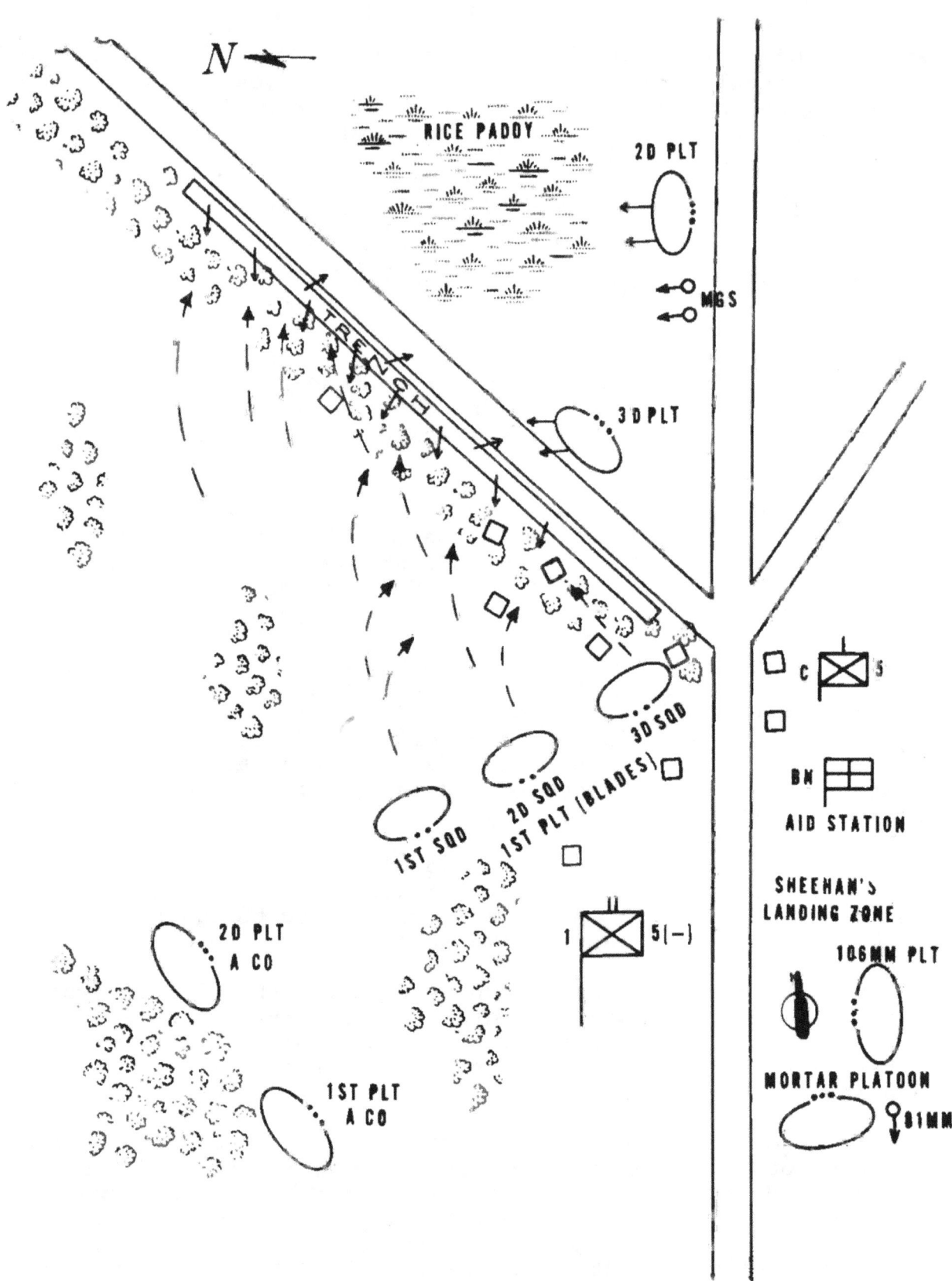

SCHEMATIC SKETCH TO ACCOMPANY "THE ASSAULT OF CHARLIE COMPANY"

Next he called up the 1st Platoon and told their platoon commander, First Lieutenant Arthur Blades, to take the hedgerow by assault. It was an understrength platoon even at the beginning, numbering only 37 men, including attachments. The 2d and 3d Squads held but six men each. It was agreed Blades would mark his progress by smoke as he went, so that the base of fire could be shifted and kept ahead of him.

Blades deployed his platoon on line to the left rear of the 3d Platoon. He pushed straight north through the underbrush with his three squads abreast, the 3d Squad on the right nearest the 3d Platoon, the 2d in the center, the 1st on the left. The platoon moved up abreast of the 3d Platoon without opposition.

The 3d Squad was guiding on a deep, narrow trenchline cut under the bushes just at the edge of the paddy. The rest of the platoon was strung out left for 60 meters. The men could not see farther than 20 meters through the maze of undergrowth, palm and banana trees, and thatched houses.

There came one of those odd lulls in a fire fight when everyone stopped firing at the same time. That was the moment Lance Corporal Palmer Atkins chose to move his squad, the 3d, into a small clearing. From less than 30 feet away a brace of automatic weapons withered the Marine skirmish line. Four of the six riflemen were struck down. The other two fell flat and returned fire.

Blades called Darling, asking for additional men so he could protect his flanks. While he was on the radio, the last two members of the 3d Squad were hit by small arms fire. Blades had lost a whole squad--three of the six casualties were dead --and had not struck a blow at the enemy. He had no idea how many enemy opposed him nor how well they were armed. He did not know, nor would he have cared if he had known, that his platoon faced the contest which characterized Marine operations at places like Tarawa, Peleliu, Iwo Jima, and Seoul: an assault against a determined, entrenched, and well-disciplined enemy.

Responding to Blades' call for help, Darling gathered a group of Marines and a machine gun crew and sent them forward.

As the action had increased in intensity, control of the company had fragmented and a distinct separation of responsibilities within the command group had occurred. This was as it should be but rarely is. Darling controlled the overall tactics and the commitments of his platoons. Gunnery Sergeant Steve Jimenez functioned as general supervisor and foreman. He pointed lost Marines in the direction of their units, organized special details to carry ammunition or casualties, and ensured that the spread of outgoing fire along the long two-platoon base stayed steady and even. The company first sergeant, Thomas J. Dockery, saw to the evacuation of the wounded. Dockery set up an aid station and evacuation point to the rear originally to handle only Charlie Company's casualties. But Lieutenant Colonel Coffman, seeing that the top sergeant had organized a system, directed that the battalion aid station be set up alongside him. Soon Dockery found himself keeping a record of all the casualties, allotting spaces on helicopters according to the corpsmen's recommendations, and keeping the battalion commander informed as the number of wounded grew. These chores he handled well.

"But my biggest problem," he said, "was holding back forward observers, logistics support people, 81mm mortarmen, engineers, company and battalion headquarters personnel, and radiomen who wanted to quit their usual job and go up to the front. Even the corpsmen who were supposed to stay in the battalion aid station were heading out with grenades and bandages."

(Within the perimeter of the battalion command group, the S-3, Major Bayard "Scotty" Pickett, had the same problem. He had to physically restrain Marines from leaving what they considered unnecessary jobs and rushing to the front.

"But, hell," the ex-All-American football player grinned. "I really wasn't too mad at them when I hauled them back. I couldn't be--I did the same thing myself.")

Dockery, a smiling Irishman and a ready talker, kept the wounded talking to the corpsmen and to each other--talking about anything to keep their thoughts away from their wounds and their bodies away from lapsing into shock. Still, one Marine died of shock before Dockery could get him helilifted out. "What got me about that one," he said, "was that his death wasn't necessary. He was shot in the elbow but a lot of guys were hit worse and made it. He just clammed up inside himself and we couldn't snap him out of it, not even by slapping him. He said he was going to die, and he did."

Darling's executive officer, Lieutenant Benigo, handled the job of getting the wounded off the field and back to Dockery. Altogether, that amounted to 38 men, but Benigo was not around for the final tally. While carrying a wounded man out of the paddy, he was struck on the back of the skull by a round which spun his helmet off and threw him flat.

"My God," he thought, "I'm dead."

Part of his scalp had been laid bare and he was bleeding hard. As if in confirmation of his own belief, he heard a voice yell, "The lieutenant's dead."

Then he thought, "No, I'm not dead."

He scrambled to his feet, picked up the wounded man again, and staggered back to the aid station. He made two more round trips, weaving in a drunken fashion and ignoring all suggestions that he get on a helicopter himself. When he returned a third time to the aid station, he was set upon and forcibly evacuated, to the last protesting he had only been scratched and the bleeding would stop at any moment.

Most of Charlie Company's wounded came from the 1st Platoon. When the reinforcements Darling had dispatched reached Blades, he placed them on his left flank, thereby freeing his remaining two squads to clear the trenchline. The 3d Squad on the extreme right having been wiped out, he sent his 2d Squad forward parallel to the trench but shielded by two houses. In this movement, two more Marines went down. Blades felt sick. Although a hard, driving man, he was close to his men and had argued insistently to keep his young squad leaders and make rank within his own platoon, not to bring in leaders from other platoons. Now fully one-third of his organic unit was down and the enemy force seemed unhurt.

Instead of falling back, the platoon redoubled its efforts. From behind the houses, the Marines lobbed grenades into the trench, while men back a few yards with Blades blasted away with automatic rifles. The platoon commander was hit in the back by grenade fragments which ripped his flak jacket. He flung the jacket off and continued to throw grenades. After a series of quick throws, his men held their fire for a moment to gauge the strength of the enemy. The opposing fire had definitely slackened, so Lance Corporal Irwin Brazzel led his three men in a dash forward to the next house in an attempt to outflank the North Vietnamese. Two automatic weapons opened up again and Brazzel and another Marine were cut down. That left two fighting men in the 2d Squad. Blades was in anguish. Brazzel, hit in the shoulder, crawled behind a house. The other Marine lay exposed and motionless. A corpsman rushed forward to help him and was killed.

Blades wasn't sure they had killed a single enemy. But the Marines were bombarding the trench with grenades and three grenade launchers and a dozen rifles. Still, two--and only two--automatic weapons replied after each fusillade.

Brazzel called to his lieutenant.

"Sir, the sniper is on the other side of this fence. I can't shoot through it but I think you can work around it all right."

Blades moved up with the 1st Squad--his last squad. The squad leader, Corporal Christopher Cushman, deliberately stood erect for a second, then dropped flat. The sniper Brazzel had warned about sprang up to fire and was shot by Lance Corporal Walter McDonald, a combat photographer who had swapped his camera for a rifle.

Next Blades had his party provide covering fire for a Marine lying wounded in a clearing. The Marine crawled into a house next to the trench and started kicking out the back wall so he could throw grenades into the trench. Hearing the commotion just above his head, an enemy soldier riddled the wall, wounding the man again. While the enemy soldier's attention was so diverted, McDonald darted around the house and dropped a grenade right on him.

The Marine assault was now gaining momentum. As the enemy fell back, three engineers attached to the platoon worked their way up the trench itself, keeping the pressure on the rear of the enemy while Blades' party pounded them from the left and Darling's base of fire poured in from the right. When the enemy, retreating to concealed positions around a tall haystack, pinned down Blades and his men, the engineers crept up the trench. Once close in, Lance Corporals Clifford Butts and William Miller raised up and fired furiously at the foliage around the haystack, while Private First Class William Joy hurled grenades as fast as he could. They blew the haystack, most of the surrounding foliage, and some of the enemy apart and forced the others to abandon the position and pull back.

The engineers, who had worked together on other operations, kept their trio intact under the intense fire. But that was the exception. The other Marines had naturally split into pairs. Clearing the trenchline became a team effort. One Marine would throw grenades while the other covered him by rifle fire. In this way, Lance Corporal William Cox and Private First Class Michael Stevenson worked their way to Brazzel and dragged him back.

Blades kept urging the men forward. He directed and the men responded. Even those who did not belong to the platoon, but who came to fight, took their cue from his leadership; such as McDonald, who later said, "I just did what the lieutenant told me to do."

There were two Marines who crawled up the trench and asked the platoon commander if they could help. Blades responded, "Yes, with grenades." At which they extracted several grenades from their pouches and held them out to him.

"Who the hell do you think I am," Blades roared, "John Wayne? Get out of that trench and go throw your own grenades!"

They did.

The M-79 grenade launcher, a key weapon in the fighting in Vietnam, ready to be fired. (USMC A187534)

The body of a North Vietnamese soldier lies near the narrow trench that was the center of C/1/5's battle during Operation Colorado. (Author's photo.)

In an action typical of many fought in the rice paddies of Vietnam, an M-60 machine gunner rises up to get a better field of fire as he supports an attack. (USMC A369433)

The platoon sergeant, Sergeant Orwin Spahn, kept an eye on the massive base of fire and as the platoon advanced, threw smoke grenades ahead to shift the fire. He stuck close to Blades. Both used grenade launchers, a weapon they found particularly effective in rooting out the tenacious enemy.

The Marines were pushing the defenders back but they still weren't sure how many there were or how many they had killed. The men could see occasional targets, however. A head or a back would poke up here or there from the trench for an instant and the Marines would cut loose. Fighting at less than 15 yards, they were sure they were dropping some but the two automatic weapons continued to blaze at them from successive positions up the trenchline. Grimly, the men dogged after the enemy.

The end came quite suddenly when the North Vietnamese ran out of trenchline at the point of the hedgerow. Blades was grinding forward on the left. Darling's base of fire was sweeping the open paddies to the right. The Marines sensed victory when some of the enemy broke and ran. Cushman saw a figure in gray khaki hop out of the trench and duck into the bushes. The squad leader waited until he moved, then shot him. McDonald nailed two more in a similar manner.

But that was all. The rest stayed and died in a roar of exploding grenades and automatic rifle fire. Blades radioed to Darling. He had to put the call through himself. In the closing minutes of the battle both his platoon sergeant, Sergeant Spahn, and his plucky radio operator, Private First Class William Brown, had been hit.

"We've taken the objective," he said.

The platoon commander limped over to the last section of the trench and peered down. It was clogged with bodies pressed side by side or laying in heaps, smashed and torn by bullets and grenades. The Marines counted 19 bodies, most packed within 15 meters of trenchline. They picked up 17 new automatic weapons and packs crammed with stick grenades and link ammunition smeared with vaseline.

The discipline of the North Vietnamese in firing just two weapons at a time had been excellent. Their positions were deep, covered, and camouflaged. A detailed map found on the body of their company commander indicated the care with which he had prepared his fire plans and drilled his men. Yet, instead of ambushing and annihilating the lead Marine platoon, they were overrun and killed.

Three factors contributed to the success of the Marines' grinding assault--Darling's plan, Blades' leadership, and the troops' aggressiveness. Especially the latter. In the opening

minutes of the attack, Blades lost 10 out of the 12 men in the
two squads first to engage the enemy, including both squad
leaders. The assault could have crumbled then and there. It
didn't. The men went on in. They weren't perfect. They made
mistakes and Blades was the first to point them out. In particular, he noted that men were wounded or killed because they
stood erect when they should have crawled. They did so because
they were tired and it was easier to move by standing. The
weight and bulk of their gear contributed greatly to this
fatigue. Still, they adapted to two-man teams and waded in
slugging, and kept slugging, until they destroyed the enemy
force.

AFTERMATH

It would be nice to close the story here, with the Marines
holding the field of battle and the North Vietnamese, beaten at
every turn, slipping away in the growing dusk, never to return.
But Vietnam isn't like that. It doesn't just end decisively.
Nor did this engagement, really.

The North Vietnamese pulled back at dark and Kilo Company,
3/5, was flown in to lend a hand, but the fight had passed.
The battalion buttoned up tightly in a circular perimeter.
Flareships kept the area lighted and massive artillery fires
ringed the battalion. Not even snipers harassed the lines.
The companies passed a quiet night, noticeable for its lack of
activity.

But for one Marine it was a night of terror. It had taken
Corpsman T. C. Long an hour and a half to crawl out from under
Donathan's body. When at last he had freed himself, it was
dusk and he hadn't the strength to move any more. He lay in
the mud with the stinging in his kneecap where the ants were
feeding on the raw flesh and waited and dozed and prayed. Sometime during the night, two North Vietnamese walked past and
tripped over him. They stopped and stripped both the body and
him of gear. Long played dead until they walked away. At times
he blanked out. Once he awoke with a terrible thirst and
crawled to a puddle close by. As he drank, he heard footsteps
approaching. He turned his head to look and was blinded by a
bright light. He blinked dazedly into the beam of the flashlight for a few seconds, then it went out and he heard the
footsteps receding. "Why didn't he kill me?" he thought.

At first light Captain Furleigh sent out a strong patrol
to find the bodies of the two missing men. This time Bielecki
saw Long, lying in a rice paddy beside the trail. They carried
him and Donathan's body back.

While Lieutenant Colonel Coffman sent out patrols to
police the battle area and pick off enemy stragglers, the press
came in to get the story. The men had little to say. To each

other they talked long and fully and eagerly. But to strangers they were reluctant to speak.

By midmorning, the patrols and outposts were engaged in desultory exchanges with enemy skirmishers and snipers. The men walked warily when they left the perimeter. It was obvious there were still many of the enemy in the area.

That was why the Marines didn't quite believe it even when they saw the helicopter land and the officers in short-sleeve utilities jump out.

"Is it?", a private first class asked his sergeant.

"Sure looks like it," the sergeant replied. "I don't know anyone else in the Marine Corps who wears four stars."

General Wallace M. Greene, Jr., the Commandant of the Marine Corps, had come to the battlefield. With him walked Lieutenant General Lewis W. Walt, commander of the Marine forces in Vietnam. General Walt had a habit of dropping in unexpectedly in unsecure areas and most of the men had seen him before and were not surprised to see him again. The feeling among the troops was that, while it was all right for General Walt to expose himself, the Commandant shouldn't do so. The generals walked the trenchline Blades' platoon had cleared and asked pointed questions about the tactics and weapons used.

Ordinarily, Buck Darling is a talkative person who can go on for hours when asked about tactics or operations. But he wasn't used to talking with generals and his cryptic words to the Commandant might be the clearest code of the Marine in combat. General Greene asked him what happened.

"Well, General," he replied, "we got into a fight with the enemy."

The Commandant then asked what he did.

"General," he said, "we killed them."

The general officers left and the battalion passed the afternoon burying enemy dead, patrolling, and resting. They were going to spend the night there and they weren't happy about it. They thought the enemy had the area plotted perfectly. The battalion commander issued to his company commanders the march order for the next morning and the hour of stand-to alert for that night.

At dusk the Marines were manning the lines in force. The sky to the west was still red. Two snipers were silhouetted perfectly against the red background as they climbed up palm trees and were dropped to the ground in a burst of automatic rifle fire by men from Bravo Company. The Marine night patrols went out and one from Alpha Company, minutes after leaving the lines, killed two more of the enemy. After this quick contact, the other patrols around the perimeter were pulled in and the battalion sat defensively, waiting for probes.

None materialized and the hours dragged by. Then, at 0350, the North Vietnamese struck. With sharp suddenness, the first 82mm mortar round exploded right on the edge of the trench where the generals had stood that afternoon. It was exact firing. Other shells dropped in, striking near the command post of Alpha Company. In the blackness a Marine cried: "My God, somebody help me. I'm hit bad. Please get me a doctor. I'm dying." Corpsmen from both Alpha and Charlie Companies raced to the man, but he died.

The battalion command center was hit hardest by both mortars and recoilless rifles. Two more men died there and several others were wounded. The Bravo Company command post was established in a storehouse near the battalion CP. A 57mm recoilless shell struck the ground just in front of it and bounced into the side of the building. The explosion collapsed the inside of the shelter yet dealt the Marines trapped within only ringing eardrums and multiple scratches.

The hut where Darling, Dockery, and Jimenez were sleeping fared better. The enemy fired at least five shells at it and all passed high. Darling lay flat and listened to the shells flutter past, each sounding like a bird trying to fly with a broken wing. In the din, he just barely heard another sound and shouted: "Shut up, everybody, lie still and listen. Try and get a fix on the sound of their weapons."

They could hear in the distance the slight but unmistakable pop of a mortar and the much louder bang of the recoilless rifle.

Battalion was way ahead of them. Hueys had been called to fly over, spot the weapons by their flashes, and destroy them. With the noise of their arrival, the hostile weapons stopped firing.

In a much less effective manner, the enemy had simultaneously hit the perimeter with a ground attack. About a squad of infantry firing automatic weapons moved toward Bravo Company's positions. The Marines on the line laid down a devastating blanket of fire and the enemy fell back and did not return.

The next morning, the battalion set out to walk the final four miles in to task force headquarters. For the first two miles they would follow the same road they had taken for the past four days. Coffman again set out a double point, with

Alpha Company on the left of Bravo Company, which guided on the road. The companies moved across the rice paddies and through the hedgerows and encountered only scattered sniper fire.

In midmorning the battalion took its first casualty. The point of Alpha Company stumbled over the tripwire of a grenade and went down with shrapnel in both legs. It was Private First Class English, the man who, during the battle, had moved so swiftly to rescue a wounded Marine. While waiting for a helicopter to evacuate English, Captain Furleigh told his radioman: "Pass the word to all platoons to watch where they walk. Keep an eye out for mines and boobytraps."

Less than 10 minutes later, Furleigh crossed through a backyard at the head of his command group to get a better glimpse of his lead platoon. He saw them spread out in a paddy on the other side of a bushline. He headed for the nearest opening and pushed aside the brush in his way. A grenade went off under him and blew him back into his radio operator. Both collapsed with multiple wounds. He was a resolute, intelligent captain who deserved a better finish to his tour in Vietnam than medical evacuation.

Coffman sent Lieutenant Blades forward from Charlie Company to take command of the company and the march was resumed. The men trudged under the hot sun across the paddies and thought of nothing in particular and said very little. They were tired and the muck of the paddies slowed their pace. Bravo Company on the right had easier going along the road and began to outdistance them. Blades, incredibly fresh, spurred them on by shouting, "Come on! What's the matter with you? Square away and walk tall, Marines. Put some pride in that step!"

That was the way the battalion walked in to the task force area, jaunty and yet tired, glad to be back and proud of themselves. One rifleman actually started whistling the Marine Corps Hymn as they neared the battalion area. "Knock that off," growled his buddy, "where do you think you are--on some grinder* back at boot camp?"

"No, man," came the reply, "but I can dream, can't I?"

So they came back for a few days rest and replenishment before going out again.

And again.

---

*grinder - Marine slang for parade ground

GLOSSARY OF MARINE SMALL ARMS

<u>Automatic</u>, <u>Pistol</u> <u>Caliber</u> <u>.45</u>, <u>M1911A1</u> - A recoil-operated, magazine-fed, self-loading hand weapon which weighs approximately 3 pounds with a full 7-round magazine; it has sustained rate of fire of 10 rounds per minute and an effective range of 50 meters.

<u>Grenade</u> <u>Launcher</u>, <u>M79</u> - A single-shot, break-open, breech-loaded, shoulder weapon which fires 40mm projectiles and weighs approximately 6½ pounds when loaded; it has a sustained rate of aimed fire of 5-7 rounds per minute and an effective range of 375 meters.

<u>Hand</u> <u>Grenade</u>, <u>Fragmentation</u>, <u>M26</u> - A hand-thrown bomb, which weighs approximately 1 pound, and contains an explosive charge in a body that shatters into small fragments; it has an effective range of 40 meters.

<u>Machine</u> <u>Gun</u>, <u>Caliber</u> <u>.50</u>, <u>M2</u> - A belt-fed, recoil-operated, air-cooled automatic weapon, which weighs approximately 80 pounds without mount or ammunition; it has a cyclic rate of fire of 450-550 rounds per minute and an effective range of 1450 meters.

<u>Machine</u> <u>Gun</u>, <u>7.62mm</u>, <u>M-60</u> - A belt-fed, gas-operated, air-cooled automatic weapon, which weighs approximately 23 pounds without mount or ammunition; it has a sustained rate of fire of 100 rounds per minute and an effective range of 1100 meters.

<u>Mortar</u>, <u>60mm</u>, <u>M19</u> - A smooth-bore, muzzle-loaded, single-shot, high angle of fire weapon, which weighs 45.2 pounds when assembled and fires an assortment of high explosive and pyrotechnic rounds; it has a maximum rate of fire of 30 rounds per minute and sustained rate of fire of 18 rounds per minute; the effective range is 2000 yards.

<u>Mortar</u>, <u>81mm</u>, <u>M29</u> - A smooth-bore, muzzle-loaded, single-shot, high angle of fire weapon, which weighs approximately 115 pounds when assembled and fires an assortment of high explosive and pyrotechnic rounds; it has a sustained rate of fire of 2 rounds per minute and an effective range of 2200-3650 meters, depending upon the ammunition used.

Recoilless Rifle, 106mm, M40A1 - A single-shot, recoilless, breech-loaded weapon, which weighs approximately 438 pounds when assembled and mounted for firing; it has a sustained rate of fire of 6 rounds per minute and an effective range of 1365 meters.

Rifle, Caliber 7.62mm, M14 - A gas-operated, magazine-fed air-cooled, semi-automatic shoulder weapon, which weighs approximately 12 pounds with a full 20-round magazine; it has a sustained rate of fire of 30 rounds per minute and an effective range of 460 meters.

Rifle, Caliber 7.62mm, M14 (Modified) - The automatic rifle version of the M14, which weighs approximately 14 pounds with bipod; it has a sustained rate of fire of 40-60 rounds per minute and an effective range of 460 meters.

Rifle Grenade, HEAT, M28 - A high-explosive, antitank bomb, fired by a launcher fixed to a rifle, which weighs approximately 1½ pounds; it has an effective range of 91 meters.

Rocket Launcher, 3.5 inch - A single-shot, open-end, shoulder-fired antitank weapon, which weighs approximately 22 pounds when loaded; it has a sustained rate of fire of 4 rounds per minute and an effective range of 273 meters against point targets.

Rocket Launcher, HE 66mm, M72 (LAAW) - A disposable, single-shot, open-end, shoulder-fired, light antitank weapon, which weighs approximately 5 pounds when loaded; it has an effective range of 250 meters.

COVER PHOTOGRAPH:

In an action typical of many fought in the rice paddies of Vietnam in 1966, an M-60 machine gunner rises up to get a better field of fire as he supports an attack. (USMC Photo A369433)

www.ingramcontent.com/pod-product-compliance
Lightning Source LLC
Chambersburg PA
CBHW080515110426
42742CB00017B/3117